In praise of *Transforming Education* . . .

"*Transforming Education* is a powerful message about the importance of providing schools where the students become acquainted with and involved in the universe, where learning and discovery takes priority over grades, where students attend school because they want to be there instead of mandated to be there. I highly recommend it to every school administrator, politician, parent, and educator."
        Doris Minick, High School Principal
        Edwards, CA

"*Transforming Education* is an exciting book because it enhances the strengths and self-esteem of the individual. It could become the long sought conceptual framework for education."
        H. Vaughn Whited, Ph.D.
        Oakland Community College
        Bloomfield Hills, MI

"*Transforming Education* presents insights and observations, convictions and suggestions for educating the total person. It could make a difference in recasting a disconnected world."
        Grace Pilon, SBS, *The Workshop Way*
        Peace of Mind at An Early Age

"What else can I say but 'Right On, Shalom, Allelujah, Amen, Hosannah!' This reader-friendly book is a must for teachers, parents, for anyone concerned about where we are headed as a society."
        Tella Sametz, Secondary School Guidance Counselor
        London, Ontario

"Asking old questions and arriving at old solutions has not worked. It is time to listen carefully to new messages such as the challenging ones Dr. LePage relates in *Transforming Education*."
        Shirley L. Henry, M.S., Life Skills Consultant
        Council Bluffs, IA

"This work is a powerful argument for reinventing education, which is necessary in order to reshape our future. *Transforming Education* could attract a new breed of teacher in the schools of education."
>Michael Whitty, Ph.D.
>University of Detroit

"Anyone who is in a leadership position *must* read this book in order to be more effective in their leadership—either in a school situation, a community setting, or in a private corporation."
>Raj K. Chopra, Ph.D., *Making a Bad Situation Good*
>Superintendent, Shawnee Mission, KS

"*Transforming Education* is an exciting work. Its suggestions for change are practical and its hope for the future uplifting."
>Randi Kennedy, Junior High Art Instructor
>Council Bluffs, IA

"This book is a breath of fresh air. The integrated curriculum including community involvement could provide students with a broad education as well as a much needed positive role in society."
>Connie Shonka, Early Childhood Education Center
>Bellevue, NE

"*Transforming Education* encourages all of us to do what we can to improve the quality of our schools. Robert Kennedy's words come to mind: "Some men see things as they are and ask, 'why?'; other men dream of things that never were and ask, 'why not?' Andy LePage asks 'Why not?'"
>Tom Shonka, Junior High Mathematics Instructor
>Bellevue, NE

"If you are a parent agonizing over the sad state of education for our children, if you are an educator refusing to burn out or collapse into cynicism, if you are a political leader needing the freshest creative thinking in education today, if you are a citizen recognizing the simple fact that education today is society tomorrow, skip all the other books and go right to the central wisdom—take Andy LePage's book to a place of solitude, and allow yourself to be drawn into the immense and joyful work of *Transforming Education*."
>Brian Swimme, Ph.D.
>*The Universe is a Green Dragon*

"The thing that struck me the most from the beginning of *Transforming Education* to its conclusion is its readability. The author's style is such that one wants to continue reading—this is not often the case in educational dissertations. It's great reading to help teachers prepare to feel fresh again!"
      Nancy Wallior, Seventh-grade Instructor
      Oakland, CA

"Thank you for renewing my beliefs and emotions about teaching. It is my hope that all educators will be fortunate enough to read this work. Its words evolve as beautifully as does a child's esteem."
      Paula Rayment Leinen, Bilingual Kindergarten Teacher
      Santa Ana, CA

"*Transforming Education* is an exciting prescription for our alien present-day educational system. If only a few of these ideas are put into practice dramatic betterment would take place."
      Charles Woodward, Elementary-grades Teacher
      Mineola, NY

"Our society's double standards create inherent problems for education. *Transforming Education* points out and defines these problems clearly in an easy to read and concise format."
      Beverly Howland, Third-grade Teacher
      Pulaski, WI

"*Transforming Education* is an exhilarating adventure into a world based on appreciation of life and all it offers. This approach to education rings with honesty and resounds with love. It's too bad the world citizenry hasn't benefited from an education in the Dr. LePage school of the universe!"
      Phoebe Revelle, High School Teacher of the
        Educably Handicapped, Oklahoma City, OK

"*Transforming Education* touches the emotions and is an illumination for all. It should be required reading for any methods class and should preface the credentialing process."
      Barbara Endres, First-grade Teacher
      Palmdale, CA

"Speaking from the position of elementary school principal in Ontario, Canada, I wholeheartedly recommend this book to my colleagues everywhere. Its title is not at all presumptuous; it very definitely has the potential of transforming education in North America. I have recommended this book as a key text for our local principals' refresher courses."
        Frank J. Saul, Principal
        Toronto, Ontario

"Dr. LePage presents a comprehensive overview of the crisis in American education and echoes the many voices of those who offer practical steps to a more positive future."
        John Graham, Second-grade Teacher
        San Francisco Waldorf School, CA

"*Transforming Education* is a practical voice of conscience needing to be heard by educators and parents everywhere. This book must finds its way—as soon as possible—to all educators for an immediate and full application of its principles."
        Gloria Crook, Founding President,
        The Robert Muller School, Arlington, TX

"*Transforming Education* echoes Paulo Freire's philosophy for liberating the learner in each individual rather than oppressing the learning through teacher-dominated methodology."
        Sr. Eileen Sullivan, SBS, High School Principal
        New Orleans, LA

"This book could well be one of the most significant books written in recent years not only for its statement of the changes that need to take place but because of the realistic manner in which the author outlines how transformation might take place without destroying the basic structure of the institution itself."
        Robert W. Reasoner, Director of the Center for
            Self Esteem
        Superintendent, San Jose, CA

TRANSFORMING EDUCATION

Andy LePage, Ph.D.

Oakmore House Press
6114 La Salle Ave., Suite 328
Oakland, CA 94611

Published by:
Oakmore House Press
6114 La Salle Ave., Suite 328
Oakland, CA 94611
(415) 531-6070

Copyright © 1987 Andy LePage, Ph.D.

The materials which appear in this book may be freely reproduced for educational/training activities (except those for which reprint permission must be obtained from the primary sources). There is no requirement to obtain special permission for such uses; however, we ask that the following statement appear on all reproductions:

> Reproduced from
> *Transforming Education*
> Andy LePage, Ph.D.
> Oakland, California: Oakmore House
> © 1987, Andy LePage, Ph.D.

This permission is limited to the reproduction of materials for educational/training events. *Systematic or large-scale reproduction or distribution—or inclusion of items in publications for sale—may be done only with prior written permission.*

Library of Congress Cataloging-in-Publication Data

LePage, Andy, 1941-
   Transforming education.

   Bibliography: p.
   Includes index.
   1. Education—United States—Aims and objectives.
2. Public school—United States. 3. School improvement programs—United States. I. Title.
LA217.L45   1987   370'.973   87.18534
ISBN 0-941079-03-1

Dedication

This book is dedicated to my father, Andy LePage, Sr., who manifests wisdom; to children worldwide, who are our precious resources; and to teachers, who are every country's national treasures.

Contents

Foreword by Assemblyman John Vasconcellos   xi

Introduction   1

1. The Legacy of Cultural Pathology   5
   The Disease of Dualism
   Education as Industry: the Death of Intrinsic Values
   The Rise of Consumerism

2. Towards Healing and Wholeness   21
   Beyond the "Banking Approach" to Education
   Beyond Conformity, Orderliness, and Predictability
   Beyond *The Nation at Risk* Report

3. The Art of Education   45
   Beauty, Leisure, and Allurement
   The New "Three R's": Reverence, Renewal, and Responsibility

4. Forgotten Values in Education   63
   Acceptance, Touch, and Trust
   Admiration and Encouragement
   Wonder, Play, Creativity, and Celebration
   Choices and Consequences

5. Enabling Educational Health   95
   Honoring Temperaments and Difference
   Developing Creative Learning Environments
   The Differently-Abled is Us

6. Revolutionizing the Curriculum   111
   Inclusive and Earth-Related
   Stimulating Young Children and Adolescents
   Learning from the School of Life

7. Transforming Leadership   139
   Lessons from the Best-Run Companies
   Transformational Leaders

8. A New Paradigm for Learning   149
   Sensing Needed Movement
   Implementing Meaningful Change in Ten Key Areas

9. Networking for Cooperation   177
   Our Interdependent and Interconnected World
   Utilizing Global and Community Resources

Acknowledgements   181

Notes   183

Glossary   199

Bibliography   209

Index   213

Foreword

Whenever institutions experience difficulty or do not work, the people in them and the people outside them usually view the institution as in the wrong. Various reasons and problems are cited, and a range of solutions is offered to get it acting in a better way. Few of us seem willing to understand that the institution does not rise or fall on one person or a few people, but that institutions are a mirror of all people.

When it comes to education, and how we view it, it must be understood that our educational institutions are a mirror of ourselves. The problems that education faces today are problems that the human faces today. The institution of education is as healthy as the human is and herein lies the root of education's present difficulties. How we view ourselves is how we "do" education.

Every one of us human beings shares two common denominators which inform our lives, choices, and behaviors: our common human nature, and our common goals. Because of our human nature we coalesce into a race, a nation, a people. Because of our common goals we want a peaceful world, safe streets, good families, good health, opportunities for education, and meaningful lives.

It is easy to think that because we are human and share common goals, we as a nation could agree on a positive plan of action in education and move with it; however, this is not the case. We humans are a diverse people, and central issues in our lives, choices, and behavior take on a diverse methodology: it becomes a question of "how?" How do we go about moving ourselves from here, where we are, to those ultimate goals we share? Logically and necessarily our selection of means depends upon our most basic assumptions about our shared human nature, for these basic assumptions will determine how it is that we humans move and are moved. And therein lies the greatest basic all of us humans do not share: we do not share a *common* belief, vision, and expectation about our common human nature.

Many, mostly traditionalists, still carry the cynical belief that we are, by nature, evil, irresponsible, and untrustworthy. This belief is gradually being countered by a growing number who believe that, instead, and to the contrary, we are naturally inclined toward becoming life-affirming, cooperative, responsible, and trustworthy. However, the traditional negative assumption has been around a long time, and modern education has been based on this from its beginning. Under this negative assumption, we logically act to repress and contain ourselves. Under the newer positive assumption, we logically act to liberate and express ourselves; even to fulfill ourselves. The most obvious form of all this is in the dualism of Descartes and western culture, and the repression of the body over the mind. In my experience, both personal and societal, it is precisely this dualism and its resultant repression—this limited view of ourselves as human—that has our world today in such disarray and despair.

The way out, the way back to ourselves and to hopefulness, health, and our full humanity, must soon be found, if we humans are to survive. That way out is to be found in re-envisioning ourselves: from negative to positive, from cynical to faithful, from repressing to liberating, from self-denying to self-fulfilling.

It is crucial that this process become explicit in our educational systems, public and private, at all levels. The underlying beliefs in people and in the educational system must become positive. Expectations regarding ourselves and our motivational processes too, must become positive. We know what negative assumptions produce in our educational systems, for every day we see children who have been crippled, some paralyzed, some even destroyed, because our common belief and vision has followed the cynical and the put-down, rather than the positive and the uplifting.

What we need, if we are to survive, is a transformation of culture, to be brought about by a transformation of education, to be brought about by a transformation of the persons who operate education, based upon a transformation of their vision of themselves and our vision of ourselves.

This book is about that transformation. It is more than an historical academic treatise; it is a cogent, crucial, practical insight, offering both a direction in which to go, and instruction in how to get there. It points out that the success of our efforts at transformation, and the realization of our human potential, depends not upon some distant redeemer — including the political leaders of our times. Rather, it depends upon each of us human beings — especially upon those of us who choose to operate within education — addressing our own personal vision of ourselves, and being willing to increase our self-esteem, even to change ourselves.

    Assemblyman John Vasconcellos
    California State Legislature
    February 1987

Introduction

In a recent poll of school superintendents in the United States money was reported to be the number one concern. Other worries, in their order of importance, were: instructional programs, teacher training programs, student's poor test scores, administrators' training, and the recruiting of good teachers.[1] One could conclude from this poll that several million dollars and a few well placed programs would solve the difficulties in education. This is not so.

Public confidence in schools has been eroding for quite some time, and public education is in crisis, but the problems in education originate at the roots of the soil of social change centuries old. Pruning the tree when the soil is polluted and the roots are dying will not result in the new growth of buds. Society has dichotomized, fragmented, and compartmentalized life and living, and it has produced an educational system born of this dualism. Hence, we pay lip service to our children, but we fail to offer them responsible education in which each child can grow, mature, and become his or her highest and best. We have substituted, perhaps unwittingly, pathology for wellness and believe we are "doing" education.

When I was cleaning the bathrooms in seminary in 1964 I began wondering why school children rarely took care of the school buildings. Staying in various dorms and buildings for the next seven years, I had ample opportunity to care for the gardens, paint the building trim, refurbish rooms, and work with whatever was necessary to keep buildings — many of them very old — alive, well, and functioning. These tasks were done along with studying, recreating, eating, and praying. There seemed to be time for everything.

Much later, as a teacher, teacher trainer, and therapist, I wondered why so many students felt unable to perform creative works and why they were so bored. I came to realize that schools were giving them specific content, but that that content did not really help them develop self-confidence, become responsible, instruct them in caring for property, or help them in their character development. Self-confidence, a sense of responsibility, caring for property, and character development were seemingly supposed to come about by some process of osmosis. Somehow, students would pick up these needed qualities from the air and begin enriching society. I came to see that education was shortchanging everyone because it was not considered an art, but rather an industry. It could train for task orientation and often do an adequate job, but it fell enormously short in helping individuals develop their personalities.

It is from meditating on these ideas and the feelings they generated, and working and speaking with teachers, students, superintendents, school board members, and people from the communities which our schools serve, that this book has been born.

To talk about American education today, it is necessary to have at least some understanding of the modern cultural period, and the major changes which brought about our present difficulties. The printing press foreshadowed an explosion in available information, but it also was effective in closing off oral tradition among people. Modern science has offered challenges and shed light on specific areas of difficulty, but it also has been effective in splintering our world and our world view. The industrial revolution helped a young nation get organized, but it did so at a terrible price to the land and people. It sought to make work an end in itself, effectively placing leisure and beauty in an adjunct relationship to be brought in when there was enough time for them, but no longer seen as part of the very fabric of living.

The American schools are beset by many problems, but the fundamental problem is cosmic in scope; that is, we live in times that are pathological — and we are part of the pathology. Our modern Western civilization began, not by inviting a traveling band of Europeans to these shores and welcoming them into

INTRODUCTION

native society; no, it began under the strain of a great duress—through the frontiersman mentality of the European settlers and of our forefathers—in which the white man took the land, moved the natives wherever he pleased, made slaves of people in other lands and brought them here, and used both the land and the people as he saw fit. Cultural schizophrenia had to rear its head; after all, it was the foundation on which our nation began. The spiritual traditions of the conquerors were not strong enough to evoke openness, beauty, and delight, either in themselves, in the land, or in the natives they found living on these shores, and so began a terrifying pathology in our development over the next four centuries.

From this difficult beginning flowed a school system which became as flawed as the culture it served. It took away beauty, truth, goodness, and the idea of an undivided land and replaced these with a fragmented, piecemeal, divvied up, partial vision in which truth is filtered and incomplete, goodness is compressed under authoritarianism, and the land is gradually parcelled out, given forty-eight names and presided over by people who sense no interrelationship among themselves, the land, and the universe. Understanding, knowledge, and humans themselves, had to be reduced to bits and pieces which could be bathed in the light of a microscope, at once to be taken apart, studied, and put back together—under the guise of education.

Transforming Education is both a practical book and a book of hope. It is about change—change not at the periphery but at the core. We might ask, "Is it too late to change?" No. But we must realize that the whole universe is interconnected and ongoing and we are part of its twenty-billion year history. Hence, for any meaningful change to occur in education, a reverence for the universe and all its life forms must be our starting point; otherwise any endeavor towards wholeness in education will be lost and only further fragmentation will prevail.

>Andy LePage, Ph.D.
>Season of Spring 1987

1

The Legacy of Cultural Pathology

The Disease of Dualism

Education needs to tap the richness and goodness of life and help students become the very best they can be; persons of intrinsic values, open to varied possibilities, at home with both toughness and tenderness, people who are not at war with themselves. This is difficult to do because of the disease of dualism which permeates our society. Dualism places people and situations in an "either/or" position. Rather than celebrating uniqueness and viewing it as part of the interrelatedness of the whole—"both/and"—dualism takes sides and views its opposite as an adversary. Hence, separation and dichotomy occur. This is manifested in various inequalities: the right over the left in politics, mind over body, capitalism over communism, science over art, civilization over nature, and men over women, to name just a few.

Education falls into this dualistic trap in failing to deal with both the inner person of the student *and* a program of learning. In those few schools where both the inner person and a program of learning have been valued, students have been able to develop to a fuller potential.[1]

Human culture and human history have also fallen into the trap of dualism, producing dullness and boredom, disease, and cultural disintegration. At certain historical times when the balance of the "both/and" was allowed, creativity was generated, the arts were respected, questioning was a method of learning, life was viewed as a search for meaning, and emotional, physical, and spiritual health allowed the culture to flourish. However, the "both/and" which produces balance has been generally absent from culture in modern times, and this absence has had devastating effects on our culture. Frederick Turner helps us understand what can happen when our humanity is thus out of balance:

> . . . we slashed and hacked at the wilderness we saw so that within three centuries of Cortes' penetration of the mainland a world millions of years in the making vanished into the voracious, insatiable maw of an alien civilization.[2]

From the 16th century on, the dominance of dualism placed European technocrat against the non-European shaman. This imbalance has become so strong in present Western culture that José A. Arguelles can say: ". . . no communication regarding world affairs is taken seriously unless it is firmly based on prevailing intellectual, power-seeking assumptions, regardless of how one-sided these assumptions are."[3] It shows up in scientific work on the brain labeling the two hemispheres "major" and "minor." It shows up historically when major developments are perceived as "masculine" and minor developments as "feminine." In our culture the left, "masculine" part of the brain, largely occupied with rational, logical, and critical processing of data, is favored over the right, "feminine" part of the brain, which uses pictures rather than words, sees patterns, and charts emotional nuances of thought.

The rise of Europe and the modern western world was seen to be related to the major or left hemisphere of the brain. This had the effect of reducing all experience to logical linear functions which could be measured and analyzed. These ideas were furthered by acceptance of the work of René Descartes. In 1619 Descartes posited certain scientific laws claiming among other things never to accept anything for true which could not be clearly known to be such; to divide each of the difficulties under examination into as many parts as possible; and to make enumerations so complete and reviews so general that one could be assured that nothing was omitted.[4]

Rather than celebrating the interrelatedness of duality, the Cartesian world view helped to separate. It placed science and religion against each other and helped establish dualism as a world view which has lasted to the present time. "Scientific" knowledge was born and grew into a body of content which became estranged from all knowledge which could not be verified empirically.

Descartes created the foundation of modern rationalism. "I think, therefore I am" would be echoed by "thinking" people for over three centuries. In the Cartesian scenario society becomes schizoid, losing contact with innate bodily responses and positing a rationale for the barbarisms which are still going on in our world—cultural, political, and economic domination.

The difficulties experienced in modern American education stem from the fact that the modern Western world has its roots in European dualisms of the 16th century and after. The tyranny of the left brain was brought to the "new world" and instead of language, astronomy, mathematics, commerce, and agriculture being balanced by poetry, music, architecture, the arts, and religion—which were part of the pre-sixteenth century world view— we suffer from the tyranny of dominance, the disease of dualism. American education believes that the former categories must be what a student "majors in"; it views the latter categories as frills available in days of flush budgets but first to go in days of lean budgets. Hence, compulsory education in America, operating for years from dominant masculine tendencies and tremendously fearful of feminine tendencies, has been greatly out of balance.

Educators can bring back the needed balance. They can begin the process of healing dichotomous thinking, and they can help to heal the antagonism between the sexes which reflects the struggle deep within the person each of us is. They can help students value both the masculine and the feminine and can help to change the pathological thinking of "either/or" which prevents dipping into both realms. Educators can help students to perceive elements as integrated, to accept the opposite within themselves, and, rather than feeling estranged from the world outside, to honor its differences. They can help students integrate the inner, psychic world with the external, linear world. Educators can help society and students work through their fear of acceptance of poetic feeling, of fantasy, of dreams, and of emotion which, says Abraham Maslow, ". . . is stronger in men than in women, in adults than in children, in engineers than in artists."[5] Finally, educators can help students and society deal with the profound cultural tendency to dichotomize, to think that in alternatives or differences we can not have both but must choose one or the other and, in that choice, repudiate the non-chosen.

The primary task for educators is, therefore, twofold: first, to work to resolve all dichotomies, to find the disease of dualism in one's personal life and heal it; and, secondly, to teach humanity to stop thinking in dichotomous ways and to teach students to start thinking in integrative ways. This involves both the changing of curricula and the changing of teacher education at the university and college level. It will require a willingness in educators at all levels to discover and accept the "shadow" side of their own personalities, to allow the integration of opposites, and to allow flexibility in their language so that the language of certainty can at times give way to the language of tentativeness.

In rooting out dichotomous thinking, educators will come to understand that there is a healthy and an unhealthy side to almost everything that can be perceived. Freud was not correct in thinking that the unconscious was only evil and therefore unhealthy. We know today from psychology and humanistic science that the unconscious is also healthy. We know that the depths of neurosis can also be the wellsprings of joy, health, and creativity. We know that nonrationality is just as necessary as rationality. We know about healthy instincts, intuitions, and even regressions. We know that within ourselves we have both the desire for selfishness and autonomy and the desire for unselfishness and surrender. If educators are to be true to their task and their responsibility, they are going to have to make sure that schools find ways to develop and strengthen autonomy in students. Research has shown that emotionally secure people have an affection for the world and for others, a trust of nature and its processes, a love for others and a desire to help them, while the insecure personality sees itself as against the world in an "either/or" dichotomy in which the other is an enemy.[6]

So it is that education has to deal first with the inner person of the student so that his or her psychological health can be maintained. Students who spend upward of twelve years in America's compulsory educational system ought to be able to develop to their fullest potential as members of the human species. Educators willing to change, willing to rid themselves of dualisms and dichotomies, willing to see into the inner person of their students, ought to be able to effect this development in their students. They can be the "hundredth monkey,"[7] aiding in the passing of the old age of dualism and the shift into the celebration of the new age of transformation.

José A. Arguelles believes that the end of an age is heralded by transformation points brought about by "heretics and visionaries":

> ... who, seizing the opportunity, maintain a middle ground between futile revolution and blind materialism . . . . Through them the present situation is articulated and the groundwork of the future is laid.[8]

Heretics and visionaries hold a dialogue with the "both/and." They comprehend the struggle of opposites and draw from each. In maintaining balance they rise above dualities and offer a transformation to a world which is neither one nor the other — neither art nor science, neither masculine nor feminine, neither major nor minor, but a new synthesis of opposites.

Education today needs to be part of the cultural paradigm shift already begun. Everything in education must be open to radical change. Educators willing to risk being perceived as heretics and visionaries will be able to make a difference. They will be able to help education become a leader in culture rather than a follower. Those who take haven in extreme caution, who prefer the "either/or" of dualism, who wish for the maintenance of the status quo, or wish to preserve the educational institution at all costs, will, unfortunately, remain part of the problem.

Education's modus operandi must always be "both/and," embracing all of life. There can be and many times there needs to be specialization in one or more areas of a discipline, but specializing cannot be interpreted apart from the whole. Education's dissecting into bits and pieces and bizarre analyzing of the parts has led to feelings of alienation, depression, loneliness, and, in some cases, suicide and murder in both students and adults.

Witness the case of the teenager in Orinda, California, in 1984 who was tried for the murder of her best friend.[9] The friend was someone who consistently "scored higher" in the pursuits of life that we have labeled very important for children. Her best friend beat her on the journalism staff; she also beat her in cheerleading. Why can't all those who feel led to be cheerleaders, lead cheers? Why won't we let those who feel led to write, write? What kind of thinking allows some to "make it" while others don't?

What message do we send those who don't make it? Only one message. It is loud, clear, devastating and deadly: "You did not make it because you are not good enough." That is discouragement in its highest form, and it happens every day in most of the schools in this country. We pay dearly to fund these dens of discouragement where our kids gradually lose almost all of their spirit and hope.

By being dualistic in our educational systems, we teach children to be takers without being givers, we teach them to view themselves in simplistic pictures of "me only" when in fact we live in a world which operates interconnectedly. Holding up math and science over art, dance, and music is dualistic. What children need is access to the real world, but education which is dualistic keeps the real world at bay. John Holt sums up the problem of dualism in education when he says:

> They take children out of and away from the great richness and variety of the world, and in its place give them school subjects, the curriculum . . . . The schools are busily cutting the world up into little bits and giving it to the children according to some expert's theory about what they need or can stand.[10]

Instead of cutting the world up into little pieces, education needs to invite inquiry on every level and to expect students to be surprised by their learning. Dissecting rather than looking for patterns which connect, locking ourselves into the dualism of "either/or," allowing musts and shoulds to cloud discovery, keep learning from taking place. Erich Jantsch says that: "Information is not transferred in one-way processes, but is exchanged in circular processes and is born new."[11]

Viewing the "both/and" and working its processes allow information to be born anew. We have to marvel at what lies before us, to speculate about phenomena, to dream about the future, to play with ideas, to say "What if? . . .," otherwise we content ourselves with the seeming comfort of the dualism. The inquiring student mind, the desire to question everything, the certainty which becomes uncertain when a new element is introduced, become lost when education is dualistic.

Unfortunately, dualism permeates all educational life. John Rigden, professor of physics at the University of Missouri-St. Louis and editor of the American Journal of Physics takes to task textbook companies and teachers for their dualistic approach in teaching science. He says that:

> Scientific knowledge is the overriding concern of textbook writers; the *quest* for that knowledge is ignored. Thus, since science *is* the quest, a distorted picture of science emerges from the pages of textbooks. Unfortunately, science education is based almost exclusively on general textbooks.[12]

Occasionally, there will be complaints about the dichotomies in textbooks, and the offending part will be remedied. Recently, California's State Superintendent of Education announced that because evolutionary theory in science textbooks has been so watered down, the state would not buy books until the publishers put out a more inclusive version. However, there is more to the textbook problem. Rigden comments about teachers who play into the problem rather than creatively solve it:

> . . . teachers . . . have designed simple interlocking logical units that enable the earnest student to rebuild, step by step, the intellectual edifice that is the current state of scientific knowledge.[13]

Because textbook authors lay out the content of science so meticulously and teachers rely so heavily on science textbooks, "the student is led with unerring precision along a smooth and straight line of development," says Rigden. "There is no mystery; there are no surprises."[14] Because of dualism, fragmentation reigns and students know exactly what is expected of them.

Students need to know more than facts from science, or other subjects; they need to know teachers, artists, and scientists as people. They need to experience the acerbic wit of Galileo, the gentle prose of Einstein, the nightmare which suggested the solution for the lockstitch to Elias Howe, the dreams which were the seeds of Mozart's music, the stories Robert Louis Stevenson concocted as a method of warding off the vivid nightmares of his childhood. Students who study the humanities usually confront the authors in these subjects, thereby learning something about them as people, but this is not so in the sciences, nor are they provided with the creative steps the scientist takes. The voices of those with competing theoretical viewpoints, as well as the voices of those who worked simultaneously on projects in other places and countries but were not first to make the claim, are forever silenced, and says Rigden, "in that deceptive hush, the assumption is encouraged that the evolution of scientific thought is smooth and unerring."[15] This dualistic view that things are smooth and unerring carries over into all of life and enables the boredom and rampant consumerism that currently prevails. When we have not been taught to look for opposites, to meditate on the mysteries of complementarity, to ponder deep within ourselves the meaning of life, and the meaning of our own lives, then life itself seems not to have meaning and, certainly, no challenges.

Dualism saps that "leading out" which education is, and in place of dialectic, paradox, and artistic expression, puts forward selected facts and figures, programming students to work in the confines of a narrow vision. Erich Jantsch, in speaking about love, makes a strong point for a dialectical, paradoxical, and artistic approach which can apply to education: "When we are in love with a person, he or she appears in unfathomable profundity and variety.... If a person appears as totally predictable, as pure confirmation of our expectations, love has died."[16]

Life *is* unfathomable profundity and variety. Educators must do all within their power to make sure schools put students in full contact with life, with all its meaning and all its interconnections and with its unlimited expressions.

Education as Industry: The Death of Intrinsic Values

There is a vast difference between an art and an industry. Art means to join, to fit together. It refers to the ability to make things, to creative work and its principles. It deals with making or doing things that display form, beauty, and unusual perception. Industry is more systematic work and deals with a product. It is usually a manufacturing enterprise or a large-scale business activity. It is certain that education (which means "to draw out") and education's goal (which is to help the student become the best person he or she can become) belong much more to art than to industry. Education brings about a joining together, helping students to make a "fit" in various parts of their lives. In our dualistic educational system it has been education-as-industry that has prevailed, and this has cost us dearly in students' failure to develop intrinsic values, in their learning experiences which have not helped them become fully human but have kept them psychologically dependent. Abraham Maslow observes that in terms of inner development of students: "Our conventional education looks mighty sick."[17] Education as industry promotes this sickness, this dichotomizing, which trivializes the human and makes him or her a compartmentalized object. This in turn leads to the death of human values.

In short, because education sees itself as an industry rather than as an art, it has used the mechanistic scientific method to study the human, and in this it has made a terrible mistake. Without human development, without the development of intrinsic values, the human is not differentiated from the machine. It is because education has seen itself as an industry that students who one day become adults make and use atom bombs, develop and carry out a technology for killing, and continue to obfuscate language. The scientific method has shown that it is possible for a person to have clear goals, be efficient, be consistent in his or her work, and be predictable. But if this person does not have intrinsic values to check against and from which to develop further humanness and personal and corporate ethics, then society becomes pathological.

Development of intrinsic values happens with development of conscience, when children hear their inner voices, learn to question, learn right from wrong, learn to follow their feelings and their thoughts. When students are not supposed to tap into their inner voices — their inner sources of wisdom — when they are not allowed to tell their dreams and have them respected, are not allowed to speak out publicly about their transcendent ecstasies, because these things are not "scientific," they repress that which speaks to them from the inside, that which is their own inner life, and which leads to the aesthetic. Unable to find the aesthetic in themselves, they necessarily cannot find the aesthetic in mathematics or in the oneness of the universe. Unable to find joy in peak experiences or in the solving of a problem, students become alienated and ultimately bored.

Education is about learning to grow as a human being. It is also about learning what to grow toward, learning what is good and bad, desirable and undesirable, learning what to choose and what not to choose, and learning about the consequences of those choices.

Since education is perceived as an industry we expect students, by some kind of osmosis, to develop values because they are told to. We expect them to keep away from drugs because we tell them they are not good for them. Without developing meaningful ways of experiencing intimacy we expect that students will delay having sexual intercourse because they are told to. Without the arts and the values inherent in the arts—music, rhythm, dance, movement—values which are so close to the psychological and biological core of the human, we expect students to become fully human. Without teaching that people and all creation are precious, we expect that children will learn to love others and all creation. Without teaching awareness of the body, and love and reverence for the body, we expect that children will automatically have positive experiences with their body. So confused are we in education that we have machines in schools which dispense junk food at whim to our children, and many high schools provide smoking lounges.

Revelation, illumination, insight, understanding, ecstasy—these are the vibrant experiences which move people, which open them to greater possibility. Yet these terms are almost forbidden in schools. So deep are the dualisms and dichotomies of the industrial model that school children are almost forbidden to have a pleasurable school experience, to enjoy themselves in the classroom. Abraham Maslow speaks of what happens to educators when schools are run according to an industrial model:

> The overwhelming majority of teachers, principals, curriculum planners and school superintendents are devoted to passing on knowledge that children need to live in an industrialized society. They are not especially imaginative or creative, nor do they often question *why* they are teaching the things they teach. Their chief concern is with efficiency, that is, with implanting the greatest number of facts into the greatest possible number of children, with a minimum of time, expense, and effort.[18]

It is of paramount importance that individual and collective creativity be tapped. But this is not going to be done in schools where teachers and administrators have plugged up their imaginations, where their creativity has been allowed to atrophy. Educators need

THE LEGACY OF CULTURAL PATHOLOGY

to ask themselves *why* they do what they do, and ponder the thoughts and feelings thus generated.

Present goals of education must change. The unspoken goal of classroom etiquette is often the pleasing of the teacher. Children learn quickly to size up situations and follow the system. When creativity is not encouraged but punished, when repeating memorized responses is rewarded, students learn to concentrate on the appropriate answer rather than to question, to ponder, to listen to their hearts. In this environment children learn exactly "how to behave" and do so. Any fresh ideas, any inner thoughts and feelings, are kept strictly to themselves. They may talk to their peers about them but never the teacher. The sadness inherent in the industrial model of education is summed up in a rather plaintive cry by John Holt at the end of his very readable book *How Children Learn:*

> This book did not change, as I had hoped it might, the ways schools deal with children. I said, trust them to learn. The schools would not trust them, and even if they wanted to, the great majority of the public would not have let them. Their reasons boil down to these: (1) Children are no good; they won't learn unless we make them. (2) The world is no good; children must be broken to it. (3) I had to put up with it; why shouldn't they? To people who think this way, I don't know what to say.[19]

Holt's words are some of the most telling ever written dealing with the results of years of education as industry. He is right: schools do not trust children to learn. They are scared stiff of children learning on their own. The dualisms of the past and the industrial model of the present are so ingrained in educators and in the educational system, that trust in the larger picture does not exist. Educators are so much a part of the power-over model (which dominates people and puts them down) rather than the power-with model (which offers freedom with responsibility and leads to self-confidence and empowerment) that they are loath to allow any other model. This is one of the saddest aspects of education which could be changed in an instant if superintendents at the state and district levels, and school boards and building principals at the local level, would take the risk of doing it. There is a double sadness here, not only that the power-over model is used on children and that trust is not part of their schooling, but that those who have the ability to change the system will not. If the educational institutions will not help people transcend the conditioning imposed on them by the culture and stop the negative imposition on present and new students, who or what agency will?

There needs to be awakened in students and in their parents a sense of brother- and sisterhood, a sense of human oneness and of the unity of all persons and of oneness with the entire creation and the universe. Education has to awaken such a sense of unity in young people that, as adults, they will hate war and do all they can to avoid it. It has to awaken within young people the power to think, to listen — to know in their minds and hearts that they are interconnected with a larger universe — and to believe and know that all life is precious and must be respected. Young people have to be awakened to the fact that humans are part of a biological evolution which is still ongoing and unfolding. They have to be awakened to listening and to learning from the inner voices which motivate them and which give them hints of their uniqueness as well as link them to the larger community of species. They have to be taught to close their eyes, to cut down noise and distractions, to turn off thoughts and put away business. They have to be taught to wait; to wait and see what happens, to trust, and to trust the processes of their very own selves.

Teachers and administrators also have to live with this kind of trust, this kind of awakening. Their joy, their satisfaction, their deep sense of accomplishment will become a model for student imitation.

There must exist an atmosphere which places the child at ease, which addresses the artist in each child, which reduces fear, anxiety, and defensiveness and permits the child to express, to act, to experiment, to make mistakes, and, most important, to love and be loved. Education which embodies the industrial model, which does not allow for the development of intrinsic values, will never reach these deeper needs.

The Rise of Consumersism

One of the societal results of education as industry is the fostering of consumerism. If the goal of a system of education is the teaching of a specific content for an industrialized society in the most efficient way possible, with little or no expectation or acceptance of creativity, then people who come through this system will have to find ways and outlets on their own to deal with their repressed emotions. Consumerism, the rampant buying of goods and services, is psychologically touted as one way of filling the need. Through consumerism people are led to believe that more is better, that unhappiness can be avoided by consuming goods and services, and that pain is something to be avoided or denied at all costs, never worked through. In each of these areas an unchecked capitalism is all too willing to manufacture the product or tout the service that can take care of any problem. Starhawk says: "Today, as long as we remain cut off from the sources of deep feeling in our lives, we remain avid consumers of packaged substitutes for feeling that can be sold at a profit to a mass market."[20]

If education were perceived as an *art,* perhaps capitalism and advertising would be perceived as arts too. This would put a different face on both these systems. They might be interested in the product *and* in the process. Moreover, our worldview might begin to change.

We have been and are involved today in a worldview that is consumeristic. Since the 16th-century European expansion into the new world, the modern white man believed that the earth was either his personal possession or that it belonged to his political sovereign, but either way it was to be used, and, if necessary, abused. Lewis Thomas says the old idea "was that the earth was man's personal property, a combination of garden, zoo, bank vault, and energy source, placed at our disposal to be consumed, ornamented, and pulled apart as we wished."[21] This consumeristic worldview is aided by an advertising industry which screams its message nonstop every hour of the day, every day of the year. It not only competes for our rational awareness but it surreptitiously seeks to capture our unconscious with its latest subliminal approaches. It is designed to grip us in such a way that we are compelled, coerced, and constrained into buying. With educational systems teaching consumerism, is it any wonder that on a school holiday, after the school day, and during much of the summer, the shopping malls of America are havens for our children? How is the exercise of hand, heart, mind, and body brought into being at a shopping center? Shopping centers are for selling and buying and that is all. With our children spending so much time there they can only pick up the erroneous messages: "You are what you own" and "More is better." Although the object of their affection can never eliminate their alienation or fill their inner void, they have not been taught this. As soon as an object is acquired, its lustre dims, its silver tarnishes, it becomes "last year's model," and the advertising industry implants the message that a "new something-or-other" will really fill the voids of alienation. It is a "no-win" situation, a maze inside a cage, going nowhere and ending only in exhaustion. Ernest Becker observes: "Modern man is drinking and drugging himself out of awareness, or he spends his time shopping, which is the same thing."[22] Matthew Fox tells us that the average high school senior — the seventeen-year-old — has seen over 350,000 commercials on American television.[23] With this constant bombardment, our children not only receive the wrong message about reality, but they have missed interaction with the real world — the world of people and relationships, of nature, of creativity, of trial and error, of celebration. Very early they feel alienated, empty, and bored, ripe for the tentacles of consumerism and its compulsions. When their sense of reality is distilled from television programs, commercials, and shopping centers, no appropriate balance can be struck because they have known so little of the joy of a leaf, the structure of a walnut, the wisdom of an inner voice, the warm arms of love. Karen Horney tells us that there is also a sadistic dimension to advertising. It plays with each of us a "game of attracting and rejecting, charming and disappointing, elevating and degrading, bringing joy and bringing grief."[24] "Advertisers," says Matthew Fox, "will stop at nothing to make us greedy for their product. They do not hesitate to destroy our language," manipulating it for their own ends.[25] Their essential message is "if you had this product, you would feel right again." Coca-Cola becomes "the real thing." Pepsi Cola rivals Coke, seemingly to care about our need to belong by telling us "we're in the Pepsi generation," or that Pepsi "is for a whole new generation." The commissioners of the Nuclear Regulatory Commission take their cue from another branch of the advertising industry by making their language the pinnacle of impersonality so they can speak of problems without any emotion. As Wendell Berry states:

> Their language and their way of thought make it possible for them to think of the crisis only as a technical event or problem.

Even a meltdown is fairly understandable and predictable within the terms of their expertise. What is unthinkable is the evacuation of a massively populated region. It is the disorder, the confusion, and uncertainty of that exodus that they cannot face.[26]

We have to search *inside* ourselves to find the treasures that we are and the values that we hold. Extrinsic ideas, inventions, and products can aid us in that search but can never be exchanged for that search and its fruit. A map is never the territory, and when we believe that it is we are in serious trouble with what we call "reality."

This does not mean that advertising cannot play a role in present or twenty-first century life. Matthew Fox says, "To announce the information that a useful product is available is a service to the community."[27] Obviously, advertising can be a plus to society. We certainly need to know what is available. But there is a demonic side to the industry in that it manipulates rather than announces, coerces rather than offers choices. Finally it titillates and trivializes everything it touches. Whereas it could join education as a teaching tool, it fails miserably; whereas it could inform and uplift us, it fosters consumerism and diminishes us all.

2

Towards Healing and Wholeness

Beyond the "Banking Approach" to Education

Education is not solely imparting knowledge. The Latin "educare" means to draw out, to lead out; also, to spend time. But because of cultural pathologies, too many schools and educators see themselves more as banks which hold a sacred deposit of knowledge and bankers who are the dispensers of this knowledge. They see themselves less as enablers to draw from students wonder, surprise, and the knowledge of connections; even less as adults who really love these children and want to spend time with them.

Three hundred years ago Galileo said: "You cannot teach a man anything. You can only help him discover it within himself."[1] There is more than a great truth here; there is a model of engagement for educators to create the environment and atmosphere whereby students are led to think, to venture, to wonder, to feel, to experience trial and error, to discover what is inside and what is outside each of them.

The ability to learn is inborn and instinctive. It develops as human beings grow and mature. Today we know that babies are not born tabula rasa but have the seeds of potential already within them. We also know that education does not take place when a model of superiority-inferiority underlies its philosophy.

When education operates on the banking approach it holds that only a certain someone can teach — a someone who is "superior" or the possessor of all or a certain amount of knowledge. Carl Rogers says:

> Here is how the politics of the traditional school is experienced: The teacher is the possessor of knowledge, the student the recipient. There is a great difference in status between instructor and student.
>
> The lecture, as the means of pouring knowledge into the recipient, and the examination as the measure of the extent to which he has received it, are the central elements of this education.[2]

The banking approach presupposes that the "superior" teacher's job is to infuse material, wisdom, enlightenment, or at least a specific content, into the mind of the "inferior" students. This becomes an automatic setup to frustrate teachers because of such mistaken beliefs and impossible goals. Witness the discouraging remarks of many teachers:

- Trying to teach Missy to learn is like trying to raise the Titanic; it can't be done!
- I'd like to drill a hole in his head and just put in today's lesson!
- I don't think Rod will ever understand math!
- I hope she marries someone who can spell for her!
- He's never going to be able to write a letter!

On and on it goes, the sad lament of teachers who believe their chief responsibilities lie principally in infusing a specific content into students. These teachers feel frustrated by what they believe are student inadequacies. Their frustrations, however, stem from their own faulty beliefs learned in America's graduate schools of education. Some of the beliefs which frustrate teachers are that they must control, that they must be perfect, that they are entitled, that they "don't count," that they are superior. Educators need to change these beliefs, but they also need to stop believing that education is only a depositing of pre-selected facts students need to "know."

Paulo Freire sees education and teachers as enabling students to observe reality critically and to deal with vital questions which lead to transformation. He comments that the banking approach to education does just the opposite:

> The banking approach to . . . education, for example, will never propose to students that they critically consider reality. It will deal instead with such vital questions as whether Roger gave green grass to the goat, and insist upon the importance of learning that, on the contrary, Roger gave green grass to the rabbit.[3]

The banking approach to education serves only to sustain the dualisms and dichotomies already in the system. Educators have to look beyond their fixed ideas, beyond limiting concepts of narrow curricula development.

They can learn much from parents' helping an infant to stand, to walk, to talk. Parents are there only to hold, support, and encourage the infant as it tries to stand; they cannot do the standing for it. When the infant falls, it tries again. Then it tries again. It even makes a game of this. Gradually, it begins to stand though for only a moment. Then it rests. It may not try to stand again for many days. Then one day it begins again. It succeeds. It stands for several moments. It learns that falling is a bonafide part of standing. It accepts this as part of its own experience; it absorbs what it can from the environment. Standing today, falling tomorrow, something else another day.

In the same way, the infant learns to walk and to talk. No one sits with the infant and actively "teaches" it to walk or to talk. If that was the only way it could learn, it would never master walking and talking. It has the inborn capacity for walking and speech, as it does for *all* learning, and so it begins "picking up" these things, actually "doing" them, responding to the environment in which it finds itself. After it masters standing, it begins to walk. That is the way it happens. We do not have to go to the infant franchise store to buy something to help it learn, nor to a specialist for a pre-packaged program of lessons, nor do parents need to rely on either their own advanced degrees or on any gurus to tell them their infant is ready to walk or talk. The infant just begins, on his or her own schedule. It neither follows cousin Gertrude nor performs because it is at the family picnic, even though many parents push their child to do this. No, it practices and develops its new activity when and only when it wants to. From doing the new behavior continually, the behavior becomes a skill. This is how *all* learning happens. Naturally. Easily. When the learner is ready. Without fatigue. Without distress. Without illness. Whether a child of the affluent or the poor. Without either a great sense of failure or a great sense of accomplishment.

The central element in enabling the infant to stand, walk, and talk, is the "being there" which parents and others do for it. Not only are parents there for the infant, they are there in loving and encouraging ways. They get excited each time the infant tries to stand. They immediately phone the relatives when the infant begins its first words and sentences. They genuinely care about its development.

Educators need to be there for students in *exactly* the same ways. They need to be there in loving and encouraging ways. They need to affirm their students, become excited, even ecstatic about their development, about their learning, at all ages and stages, at all grades. They need to become people of dialogue, genuinely listening with their ears and with their hearts, and responding out of genuine caring, warmth, and affection. Their dialogue with students has to speak the conviction that teachers and educators want the highest and the best for each of their students. Paulo Freire speaks of the need for educators to be able to carry out this dialogue with students — to be able to encounter them as human beings, connected with them and their world, their problems and joys. He poses a central question about the educator's worldview and the banking concept of education:

> How can I dialog (sic) if I always project ignorance onto others and never perceive my own? . . . . How can I dialog (sic) if I consider myself a member of the in-group of "pure" men, the owners of truth and knowledge, for whom all non-members are "these people" or "the great unwashed"?[4]

These questions have become central for all educators. When administrators and teachers lack humility they cannot hold a genuine dialogue. They become "the learned" rather than co-learners with all on the journey of life. This does not mean that teachers and students have equality of knowledge. It simply means that if teachers view themselves as their students' superiors they automatically look down on their students, thereby becoming incapable of drawing them out. Moreover, when dialogue and communication are missing, discipline becomes a problem. John O. Stevens says:

> Anything you can do to increase communication in your class will reduce your need to impose order by authority, and reduce the student's need to rebel against that authority. The class will become more a place for listening and learning, and less a place for fighting and antagonism.[5]

Dialogue increases communication. When one person provides others with his or her true thoughts, feelings, intentions, and actions, this self-disclosure becomes the fertile breeding ground for trust. When the listeners listen in a spirit of openness, of non-judgment, of mutuality, the trust becomes reciprocal. Feedback, which helps students make connections with fundamental knowledge, can take place. It can be heard because no one has an "agenda" for the other; the vested interest is in the whole group's learning.

Dialogue prevents the banking concept from taking hold in educators' thinking. It helps them become enablers of the culture by getting the culture to ask itself brave and tough questions. Neil Postman and Charles Weingartner observe: "A school is good when it moves away from valuing memorization and ventriloquizing and moves towards valuing question asking, problem solving, and research."[6] The English philosopher and historian Thomas Carlyle takes this further, showing what it does for the culture.

> The great law of culture is to let each one become all that he was created capable of being; expand, if possible, to his full growth; and show himself at length in his own shape and stature, be these what they may.[7]

If one of education's goals is to help "each one become all that he was created capable of being," then teachers and educators have to allow the process of asking tough questions:

What policies do we need to change so that our planet can be restored?

What can we do to help establish a viable peace in our global village?

What changes need to be wrought in our political system so that power-over mechanisms can be lessened and finally removed?

What is necessary for us to act responsibly towards all creation?

TRANSFORMING EDUCATION

What changes does our culture need to make to see death and dying as a natural part of the life cycle?

How must our industries change so that they can become more humanized?

What changes need to be made in our economies so that parenting and family life can be enhanced?

How can the free-enterprise system change so that it will give equal access to all?

What are the necessary prerequisites for us to lessen violence?

What other economic systems can shed light on our own system?

How can we take compulsion out of money-making?

What needs to be done to make the world economy more equitable?

What could be the accomplishments of a world-wide economy?

What role does pleasure play in our coming to maturity?

How can sexuality be restored to its holistic sense?

What learning can our native American brothers and sisters share with us?

How can we have a tax structure which is not only fair for all, but to which people would gladly contribute?

What changes do we need to make in our employment practices so that the worth of all people will be recognized?

How can we tap the artist in each of us?

How can our prisons be humanized?

How can high technology be given a human face?

What do we need to do to become celebrators?

How can we encourage creativity in our work?

What would a meaningful redefinition of our major institutions — law, medicine, architecture, science, the humanities — look like?

How do we respond meaningfully to interstellar space?

How can we repair our cracked human soul?

These are some of the tough questions which can excite dialogue between students and teachers. Grappling with these and other meaningful questions which dialogue itself will produce will lead to far more understanding and enlightenment than rehashing boring details in updated language. "Through dialogue," says Paulo Freire, "the teacher-of-the-students and the students-of-the-teacher cease to exist and a new term emerges: teacher-student with students-teachers." This means that the teacher too becomes a learner, and teachers and students together "become jointly responsible for a process in which all grow."[8] He states further, "the humbler they (teachers) are, the more they will learn."[9] And he speaks of the "unjustifiable pessimism" educators will have toward human beings and toward life if they are without dialogue:

> It is to lapse back into the practice of depositing false knowledge which anaesthetizes the critical spirit, contributes to the 'domesticating' of human beings, and makes cultural invasion impossible.[10]

Dialogue awakens such an awareness and aliveness that students will never be lulled to sleep by the voice of an "expert." Rather, with their teachers, they will go forward together to develop a critical attitude, seeking the contraries, searching the deep, envisioning new connections, looking for wider limits of the spectrum, always ready to make a new synthesis. This is "being with" in action. The questioning, the learning *with* each other, the mutuality felt, the understanding fostered the cooperation encountered, creates transformation in the culture. It makes possible what Rosemary Reuther calls for when she says: "Society must be transfigured by a new type of social personality, a new humanity appropriate to a new earth."[11]

Beyond Conformity, Orderliness, and Predictability

Education and schooling need to be more like a community gathering center, suggests John Holt, "a place where people come together to do the things that interest and excite them the most."[12] To do this, education will have to give up its fundamental ideas of conformity, predictability, and orderliness.

Not only does predictability destroy individuality, it also seriously lowers the opportunity for diversity and the acceptance of differences, and makes life frightfully dull. Ask elementary, middle, and high school students today about their lives and you hear a chorus sung nationwide: We are bored. Life is boring. School is boring. Home is boring. TV is boring. Work is boring. Riding a bicycle is boring. Raking leaves is boring. Taking a walk is boring. Painting a fence is boring. Shoveling snow is boring. Planting a garden is boring. Watering the lawn is boring. Fixing anything broken is so boring they can't even bring themselves to envision it. For our young people boredom has become a national work, a way of life, of passing time.

This is what the banking approach to education does to our children: it bores them. It offers no creativity, no challenges, no in-depth study, no mystery, no mastery, no hope, no confidence, no trust, no vision. With nothing to stimulate their sense of awe, with no invitation to the land of the unknown, with no call to the vista of uncharted seas, our children do the only thing possible: they become bored. Alfred North Whitehead suggests our methodology in education is too narrow:

> We are too exclusively bookish in our scholastic routine. The general training should aim at eliciting our concrete apprehensions, and should satisfy the itch for youth to be doing something . . . . In the Garden of Eden Adam saw the animals before he named them: in the traditional system, children named the animals before they saw them.[13]

American education does not satisfy; rather, it is very predictable. It trains large numbers of students to be unreflecting followers of the status quo. No wonder many of our young become bulimic or overweight. No wonder many of our kids can't read, can't spell, can't think, can't fill out the simplest of forms, can't talk about their sexuality, their love lives, their feelings, their hopes, their joys, their frustrations. We have predicted not only what they would be, but *how* they would be.

Some time ago there was a movie called *The Stepford Wives*, which dealt with the husbands' programming of their wives in a certain town. These wives blindly respond to pre-set commands; they smile and say frightfully dumb things as they carry out their "chores." A sequel could be made called *The Stepford Schools,* for our educational system is as programmed as were the wives of that town. Schools have taken a toll on our kids. With little or no sense of awe, of self- and other-admiration, of self- and other-respect, of the consequences of their actions and behavior, of reverence, how could students be anything but bored?

To foster predictability and maintain the status quo, schools inaugurate patterns of rigidity which they call orderliness. Order is a necessary component of creativity, but the orderliness spoken of here is order taken to an extreme. It has worked quite well, and most of us have been its all-too-willing students. Presently, our nation seems overwhelmed with this orderliness. Witness the phenomenal growth of the computer industry as computers organize data. Browse through any office supply store and find scores of aids to help us organize office, home, life, planet. Observe the proliferation of time management experts who sweep into our lives and promise to help us wrench fifteen extra minutes from an already frenetic pace if we will only follow their proven methods of tidiness and orderliness. Advice is legion: return phone calls all in a block, handle paper only once, make decisions decisively, look over the order of tomorrow at 3:30 P.M. today. We are so compulsive about order that we put rigidity into our leisure and rest, thereby robbing these terms of any possibility of surprise, of wonder, of refreshment. So orderly and predictable are we that leisure and rest are now meaningless forays into a "fun-filled weekend" complete with hours spent either crawling or speeding on the nation's highways.

Obviously we have learned these tenets of orderliness somewhere. One wonders where? In school, of course! Although the seeds of orderliness may have been planted in the home, the rigidity of orderliness escalates excessively in school. It begins in first grade when we are "grown up" enough to sit in straight chairs in straight rows in square classrooms in perfect order. Which class is cited as "best" by traditional principals? The class that is lined up "perfectly," doesn't make a sound, has the room in obvious order, and speaks only when spoken to. And many teachers feel compelled to maintain this rigidity for fear of being reproved by the principal. "Keep the waters smooth; we don't want even a ripple, much less a wave. Create the illusion that everything is going smoothly," states a teacher about what he has been told.[14] In making a demigod of order we have with one fell swoop placed most of our students in a straitjacket from which there is no accepted release. Though some refuse the clothing and thereby do not have to be released, and others gain release by antisocial actions, or much later through therapy, most buy into order under the guise of good behavior. Conditioned for so long by this ruse, many people carry it throughout life as a personal compulsion. Good teachers, aided by good parents, reinforced by good clergy — all these people who have been so damnably "good" have influenced us so strongly, that creative juices are watered down by the mediocrity of orderliness. Any wonder why all of us feel personally so powerless, so put down, so used, so unable even to see the flowers, much less take time to smell them?

The rigidity of orderliness keeps students from developing their personal power, which is a key condition for dealing with growth in self-esteem. Without this sense of growing personal power we do not feel able to be in charge of ourselves. The word "power" comes from the Latin, "posse" which means "to be able." It is an energy that comes from within. Power is the energy inherent in a seed waiting to mush-up through the soil and begin its process of growing into a plant or a tree. Power is the energy inherent in a kernel of corn waiting for just the right amount of heat to pop and become a delectable treat. Power is the energy in a person waiting in the wings for the time to blossom forth. All of us have this power within, an inherent gift which waits only to be called forth. Starhawk observes that the possibilities inherent in personal power make such an enormous wellspring that they could serve to transform the culture:

> A true transformation of our culture would require reclaiming the erotic as power-from-within, as empowerment . . . . It is the realm in which the spiritual, and the personal come together.[15]

Because of the cultural and educational pathology of the past and present, many people come to see themselves generally as "not being able." After the industrial revolution, more and more people came to "know their place," which was to do as they were told and rarely, if ever, to give their opinion. This further repressed their personal power. Power, which gets learned in the everyday situations of making choices, moves forward with little victories in which students gradually learn to feel powerful.

Education can do much to help empower students. It can begin by giving them access to tools and skills: access to libraries, museums, information, to the inner sanctums of business, to government and its agencies, to industry and the media, to parks and national wildlife refuges, to lakes and streams, oceans and mountains, field and tundra, to outer space and to futuristic planning. Through ritual, education can help them deal with life processes and rites of passage. Through the scientific method, it can teach them to question and to have "peak" experiences. Through viewing education as an art, it can help them express their creativity. Modern Americans especially need to know the empowering processes of the past. What empowered people in the twelfth century to plan, build, and bring to birth the Cathedral at Chartres? What inspired the building of Mont St. Michel high atop a rock in a sea called Peril?[16] What were the factors which brought about the Renaissance?

When education is willing to move away from the extremes of conformity, orderliness, and predictability, it can call forth in students a most powerful response to life. It can move us beyond that which trivializes, bring wholeness into our lives, transform our government, and heal our society.

Beyond the *Nation at Risk Report*

On August 26, 1981, Terrel H. Bell, the newly appointed Secretary of Education in the Reagan administration created an eighteen-member panel called the National Commission on Excellence in Education. He directed it to examine the American educational system and recommend reforms by April of 1983. The Commission sought papers from a variety of experts in education, conducted six public hearings, two panel discussions, a symposium, and heard testimony at a series of meetings around the country. It solicited letters from those with opinions about needed reforms and descriptions of notable educational programs. After twenty months of work, its conclusions were published as an open letter to the American people, entitled "A Nation At Risk."

TRANSFORMING EDUCATION

From its introduction on April 26, 1983, the Nation At Risk Report was greeted cautiously by educators. The Executive Secretary of the Iowa Association for Supervision and Curriculum Development was quite candid in his remarks to Association members: "Caution should be observed in overreacting to this report either in a positive or a negative manner."[17] Perhaps he sensed what other educators sensed, that the underlying approach of the Commission was the all-too-familiar government and societal dictum: "there's a problem, let's fix it."

Reform of the educational system is touted throughout the report, but it is precisely because the work of the Commission was so predictably dualistic that the reforms suggested cannot transform education. Henry Barnes, a longtime educator teaching in New York, said of the suggested reforms: "The Nation At Risk Report called for the 'three T's': toughen up, tighten up, and tax 'em up."[18]

On the positive side, the report does help focus on the fact that our nation's educational system is in trouble, but perhaps that is its only real contribution. It misses the larger questions underlying the possibility of transformation:

Is our present society itself part of the problem?

What characteristics of American culture are healthy and health-producing, and what are unhealthy and pathology-producing?

How do individuals grow in our society?

What is the present condition of American family life?

What vehicles are in place or need to be constructed so that family life and the schools can work together?

What are our society's values and how are they transmitted?

What characterizes America's ethics?

How is leisure practiced in America?

What constitutes America's compassion and sense of justice?

How do Americans play?

How do people in our society honor the natural environment?

What characterizes the individual American's interaction with non-human creation?

What role do the arts play in the development of our citizens?

What are the principles that control decisions about funding in America?

What is the country's definition of education?

What are the underlying problems of a "latchkey" society, and how will assigning "far more homework than is now the case" possibly be carried out in this society's present condition?

These are only a few of the questions that need to be discussed when the "National Commission on Excellence in Education" is convened to study the educational system.

The report cites some of the problems already known, but falls short in stating alternatives to deal with those problems. For example, the report says:

> The educational foundations of our society are presently being eroded by a rising tide of mediocrity that threatens our very future as a nation and a people . . . . We have even squandered the gains in student achievement made in the wake of the Sputnik challenge. Moreover, we have dismantled essential support systems which helped make those gains possible.[19]

This is true, but the Commission looked only at the surface of the situation. What would happen to the "educational foundations of our society" if educational planning included the next seven generations, or if our schools had access to all the materials, all the teachers, all the aides, all the funds they needed? The "rising tide of mediocrity" is initiated and perpetuated by the double message spoken to all school districts: "Be the best, make the best available to the students, get motivated teachers, tell them they are professionals — and insist they are not dedicated when they question their sub-standard wages."

The gains in student achievement made in the wake of Sputnik came about because Congress funded the project quite heavily — that was the "essential support system." Once more there was a problem that needed fixing. Little planning of any kind goes on at the federal level in America; instead, the funding of political "solutions" substitutes for planning. This happens in education, too. The initiation of the Apollo project was a political and educational response to our country's research and development

TRANSFORMING EDUCATION

teams' having been caught napping. If Sputnik had not been launched it is doubtful that an increase in science programs would have been funded.[20] The challenge to Sputnik was addressed precisely in the same way as the crisis in education: "there's a problem, let's fix it."

The report states:

> Our society and its educational institutions seem to have lost sight of the basic purposes of schooling, and the high expectations and disciplined effort needed to attain them . . . . That we have compromised this commitment is, upon reflection, hardly surprising, given the multitude of often conflicting demands we have placed upon our Nation's schools and colleges.[21]

Our nation's schools and colleges *have* had "conflicting demands" placed upon them. Many schools and colleges are not known for planning for the future because they are struggling to hold the line on next year's budget while facing this year's budget cuts and loss of programs and services. This goes on year after year. Schools rarely enjoy such a thing as a budgetary surplus, and because of patchwork financing, it is very difficult to give permanence to curriculum and personnel. In addition to this, politicians love the theme of family life, and whenever statistics are cited that show the family to be in trouble, they make promises to the body politic regarding education which cannot be kept. Rather than communicating with the people about ways to strengthen family life and what changes need to be made in government and society to achieve this aim, politicians tell the schools to take over another essential service, such as feeding children breakfast, and the schools all too willingly comply. Soon more time is spent deciding whether ketchup is a vegetable in a school cafeteria than how we adults are relating to our children both at home and at school.

The report states two underlying dualisms when it speaks of the risk our nation faces: first, we are told that "History is not kind to idlers," and secondly, that "The time is long past when America's destiny was assured simply by an abundance of natural resources and inexhaustible human enthusiasm and by our relative isolation from the malignant problems of older civilizations."[22] This is typical industrial thinking. Chapter 3 of this book discusses why society must have leisure as a basis for its health. Some idleness is a blessing. To say that "history is not kind to idlers" suggests the Commission's underlying message that America is less competitive and less able to bend the will of the world, and that this is bad. The Commission rightly states the "time is long past when America's destiny was assured simply by an abundance of natural resources . . . ." But the Commission seems to have little or no understanding as to why it is making that kind of statement. Some questions need to be asked:

> What have our children been taught in school concerning the natural environment?
>
> What does abundance mean?
>
> Why do we continue to produce toxic waste?
>
> How do we live cooperatively with ourselves, other cultures, and the rest of creation?
>
> Why have we allowed political and commercial interests to rape and pillage our resources?
>
> What did our founding fathers do to the original inhabitants here who resided quite peacefully on this continent and who gave thanks to their Great Spirit for the privilege of being selected to watch over and protect the sacred environment?

Simply to state that we are running out of resources and not to try to understand why it is happening and our own role in the process is to miss the possibility of transforming education and ourselves.

The report goes on to make several "leaps" by stringing together various insights:

> We need to improve on the slim competitive edge we . . . (still) retain in world markets . . . . Learning is the indispensable investment required for success in the information age we are entering . . . . Our concern . . . goes well beyond matters such as industry and commerce. It also includes the intellectual, moral, and spiritual strengths of our people which knit together the very fabric of our society.[23]

Concerning our "slim competitive edge" in world markets, education has an excellent opportunity to research deeply and communicate openly about how we can exist, learn from, and cooperate with the rest of the world and enable *everyone* to make a profit. We have to realize that we are in more than an "information age"; we are also in an age of relationships. We are in an age of care and concern for each other and our environment, an age of wanting quality in our lifestyles and of compassion towards ourselves and other cultures.

What are "the intellectual, moral, and spiritual strengths of our people"? How does education address these strengths? In present day public education it is difficult to find these strengths discussed or debated, either orally or in print. Because of cultural and educational pathology, a dualistic approach of separation and alienation prevails, keeping any discussion of morality or spirituality out of public education and confined to sentimentality in the nation's mainline churches. When education sees its rightful mission—to draw out all that is in the human, to let the mind of the universe speak to us, to inform via the presentation of all sides of a question, to allow meaningful thought and debate—then it, along with industry, government, the professions, and the churches, will be discussing morality and spirituality.

Without realizing it, the Commission supports this pathology when it says: "For our country to function, citizens must be able to reach some common understanding on complex issues, often on short notice and on the basis of conflicting or incomplete evidence." Why must understanding come on short notice? To what god are we paying obeisance that "understanding" must come about on the basis of conflicting or incomplete evidence? Dwight Allen says that as a nation, "we are some of the very few people in the world who will vote on anything, not having the slightest understanding, knowledge, or evidence of knowing what the issues are."[24]

The Commission amply documents the educational dimensions of the risk and produces a litany of problem areas. Some of their findings are:

> International comparisons of student achievement. . . on 19 tests. . .(comparing ourselves with other industrialized nations), [found that] American students were never first or second, and. . .were last seven times.

> Some 23 million adults are functionally illiterate by the simplest tests of everyday reading, writing, and comprehension.

> About 13 percent of all seventeen-year-olds in the United States can be considered functionally illiterate . . . . Minority youth may run as high as 40 percent.

> Average achievement of high school students on most standardized tests is now lower than 26 years ago when Sputnik was launched.
>
> Many 17-year-olds do not possess the "higher order" intellectual skills we should expect of them. Nearly 40 percent cannot draw inferences from written material; only one-fifth can write a persuasive essay; and only one-third can solve a mathematics problem requiring several steps.
>
> Between 1975 and 1980 remedial mathematics courses in public four-year colleges increased by 72 percent and now constitute one-quarter of all mathematics courses taught in those institutions.
>
> The Department of the Navy . . . reported . . . that one-quarter of its recent recruits cannot read at the ninth-grade level . . . .[25]

The Commission quotes educational researcher Paul Hurd saying "We are raising a new generation of Americans that is scientifically and technologically illiterate."[26]

The strength of the Commission's Report is that it is accurate. But educators, government, business, the professions, churches, parents, students, and taxpayers need to work together to begin to see the problems in proper perspective, that is, from the viewpoint of interrelationships, and then devise ways to address them and solve them. One can agree with Paul Hurd that the new generation of Americans may be scientifically and technologically illiterate; however, it must be remembered that oral tradition, the arts in general, the art of storytelling, the art and science of thinking—all of which support literacy—have been in decline since the birth of the industrial age.

Accountability at many levels of life is missing in our culture. Colleges that have accepted students who could not read or write and did not help them to correct these situations have performed a disservice to those students, to the college itself, and to the country at large. Here again the Commission misses the interrelatedness of education. Those high schools which have not been accountable have also cheated students, teachers, and the country. They have short-changed education as a whole. Those superintendents, principals, and college educators who have allowed this have done so because of their inability to lead, to take risks, to be honest about their beliefs, to stand up to state legislatures and federal bureaucracies. The Commission speaks of this disservice:

> On the personal level the student, the parent, and the caring teacher all perceive that a basic promise is not being kept. More and more young people emerge from high school ready neither for college nor for work. This predicament becomes more acute as the knowledge base continues its rapid expansion, the number of traditional jobs shrinks, and new jobs demand greater sophistication and preparation.[27]

The Commission goes on to say that although these difficulties persist there is a positive side. The problems themselves can become "a unifying national preoccupation."[28] While this may be true, it seems quite typical of government commissions to deal with crises only, rarely with prevention. The drug problem is an example, and birth control is an acute example. Instead of welcoming dialogue in sex education with our young students, instead of having caring teachers interact with parents to make the biological and emotional aspects of sexuality part of classroom and home instruction, parents and educators have chosen to ignore this essential part of education. To further dichotomize, the government slashes funds to educational institutions such as Planned Parenthood and yet funds teenage parents and their offspring through welfare payments. Education and government support this repression in the hopes that the crises of teenage pregnancy and children raising children will go away. The ostrich approach has never worked and never will work. However, it allows timid "leaders" in the field to vacillate, be vague, and write reports on excellence in the schools without paying the price of deepening their own personal values.

The Commission is deep within the industrial model when it confuses performance with excellence. It believes the greater the productivity, the greater society will be. "Excellence characterizes a *school or college* that sets high expectations and goals for all learners, then tries in every way possible to help students reach them."[29] This is management telling workers what they, the workers, will do. It is hierarchical and rests on the assumption that a few know the needs of the many. It is an example of the "banking approach" to education. It keeps students and teachers from thinking, from being creative, from making and learning from mistakes. The report says further that "our goal must be to develop the talents of all to their fullest."³⁰ Education based on the industrial model precludes this lofty ideal from taking place. It does set up standards of mediocrity which make most students and teachers passive, easily manipulable by special interest groups in government, business, and education who would like society to conform to their manipulative ways.

The Commission speaks of the possibility of transformation in education when it speaks of the need for a "learning society":

> At the heart of such a society is the commitment to a set of values and to a system of education that affords all members the opportunity to stretch their minds to full capacity, from early childhood through adulthood, learning more as the world changes.³¹

One wishes the Commission would have been as eloquent in saying how this is to take place. Certainly adding thirty or forty days to the school year is not the answer. Nor is increasing homework for students presently unwilling or unable to do homework the answer. To stretch minds, other scenes have to be evaluated: what needs to be said of parents who are rarely at home because of work? What about homework presently assigned that is not challenging or personally rewarding? What of the destruction of intrinsic moral values through television and consumerism?

The Commission states that there should be a coherent continuum of learning and admits, "we have none, but instead an often incoherent, outdated patchwork quilt."³² They have named the difficulties well. However, all that is offered for reform is tired explanations which come in the form of "Findings and Recommendations Regarding Content, Expectations, Time, and Teaching."

The Commission defines expectations "in terms of the level of knowledge, abilities, and skills school and college graduates should possess." Expectations "also refer to the time, hard work, behavior, self-discipline, and motivation that are essential for high student achievement."³³ Its first expectation is "by grades, which reflect the degree to which students demonstrate their mastery of subject matter."³⁴

Grades have rarely reflected the degree of mastery of subject matter. Educators have known this for years. Grades usually reflect a student's ability or inability to take a test, and that is all. Rarely is there a celebration of knowledge in a test, or any nuance of learning, or any shared knowledge. Even more rarely do tests test the student's "time, hard work, behavior, self-discipline, and motivation"; rather they reflect the ability to give out certain material usually based on "closed-ended questions," questions which elicit yes-or-no, true-or-false answers, and letter or number matchings. Even essay questions leave much to be desired. Tests are poor criteria by which to judge learning; there is nothing of the arts, no fun, no play in tests as schools presently use them, yet this is what the Commission on Excellence believes should not only be continued but strengthened.

Much can be learned from driver education in which the State tests a student's *experience* rather than his or her ability to quote the safety laws. Students get excited, even passionate, about their driving, and they spend much time in reflection before their road test. Few students—and often fewer teachers—get excited, passionate, or spend much time reflecting about most tests given in America's public schools today.

The report also mentions that expectations are expressed to students "by the difficulty of the subject matter students confront in their texts and assigned readings."[35] Why must commissions, educators, and people in general carry the belief that learning must be difficult? This is a left-over of the Puritan ethic that holds that to be rewarding life must be difficult. Furthermore, few students will confront difficulty in textbooks, save the difficulty of either understanding them because they are so poorly written, or the yawns they engender because they are so empty and boring. The Commission reported that many texts have been deliberately "written down" by their publishers to meet the perceived abilities of students "in response to perceived market demands."[36] One wonders why schools insist on buying them.

The report mentions that "'minimum competency' tends to become the 'maximum,' thus lowering educational standards for all."[37] This is true, but what will help competency is not the addition of homework and hours in school. Rather, it is a comprehensive plan based on personal and mentor relationships between students and teachers from which hours in school and homework will automatically flow. Children learn some things from peers, but their ability to grow in personal maturity comes about from their relationships with older generations. Yet mentorships and student-teacher relationships are not even mentioned in the report. When industrial processes—such as the banking approach—are applied to an art such as education, the inherent message is: "I, God, know what is good for you. Do it only this way. Do it now. Do it right ('my way'). Don't ask questions, and don't even think of learning as something shared between students and teachers." The Commission underscores this approach when it says: "In many schools, the time spent learning how to cook and drive counts as much toward a high school diploma as the time spent studying mathematics, English, chemistry, U.S. history, or biology."[38] Again and again, dichotomy prevails in the thinking of the Commission. They seem to be saying that the "real elements of education" are the old "three R's" and that skills such as cooking, which is more difficult to learn at home in fast-food America, or driving, which is necessary because almost all of today's students will be driving daily the rest of their lives, are merely add-ons.

Concerning teachers themselves, the Commission found that few academically able students are being attracted to the teaching profession and that teacher preparation programs across the country need substantial improvement. They also found that the professional working life of teachers is on the whole unacceptable and that a serious shortage of teachers exists in key fields.[39]

More academically able people will be attracted to the teaching profession when the profession sees itself and is seen in a professional light. As long as lotteries are devised to pay teacher salaries, as long as cities and districts refuse to fund education, as long as federal bureaucracy speaks a double message of federal guidelines but no federal money—as long as these conditions prevail, there will be little professionalism.

In January, 1986, the school teachers of Oakland, California, called a strike. They had been working for more than half a year without a contract. The City of Oakland refused to budget more money for schools, although $30 million had been made available to the Oakland Athletics baseball team to ensure that the A's would not move. Quite simply, many major cities do not care enough about education because they do not see it paying off in increased revenues. This mentality places the teaching profession in an adversarial position, constantly needing to justify its existence and its expenditures. In this sense the teaching profession ceases to be a profession. One does not see legal and medical professionals scrambling for funds or supplementing their income through part-time jobs. Nor is the Navy, the Army, or the Air Force funded by lottery. Until the Commission on Excellence in Education and other specially empowered educational watchdog groups begin wrestling with the real issues rather than making vague statements, until those in power take the risk to look at transformation rather than reformation, until citizens can have full input in the educational process, and until educators themselves say "No more," teacher salaries will continue to be dependent on whim and the prevailing winds. Teachers will continue to be seen as para-professionals rather than as the national treasures that they are.

The report states in its recommendations that ". . . we refer to public, private, and parochial schools and colleges alike. All are valuable national resources."[40] One wonders why the private and parochial schools and colleges alike are not equally funded, or why this possibility is not discussed in the report. What do the Commission members mean by their words "valuable national resources"? In his book *Standing By Words,* Wendell Berry says of the Nuclear Regulatory Commission deliberations:

> . . . the commissioners take refuge in the impersonality of technological procedures. They cannot bear to acknowledge considerations and feelings that might break the insulating spell of their "objective" dispassion.[41]

The charge against the members of the Nuclear Regulatory Commission could be brought against the members of the Commission on Excellence in Education. For they, too, take refuge in the "impersonality of technological procedures." They too are loath to "break the insulating spell of their 'objective' dispassion."

There is very little of the human in the Excellence Report. The Commissioners have walked the political line and said nothing offensive. Nor is there anything greatly challenging to government or citizens. There are challenges presented to the teaching profession, but the foregone conclusion is that funds for these challenges will not be made available. Therefore only minor changes are possible, and educators will once more be teaching with their hands tied behind their backs. The Commissioners' mention their common expectation of students: "We must demand the best effort and performance from all students, whether they are gifted or less able, affluent or disadvantaged,

TOWARDS HEALING AND WHOLENESS

whether destined for college, the farm, or industry."[42] The rhetoric covers everyone, but, much like political promises, "best efforts" are at best vague; and furthermore, if they are defined and accepted, educators will have to spend a long time looking in the educational pot for funds for these "best efforts."

The report recommends all students who seek a diploma have a foundation in the "Five New Basics" to be taken during their four years of high school. These include: four years of English; three years each of mathematics, science, and social studies; one-half year of computer science. For the "college bound" two years of foreign language are "strongly recommended."[43] The Commission spent twenty months coming up with this remarkable curriculum. What about the arts and the humanities? What about decision-making skills so necessary during puberty and teenage development? What about the realm of the "right brain"? The Commissioners bring in the arts almost as an afterthought, using language that has all the strength of a fly in cold storage: "A high level of shared education in these Basics, together with work in the fine and performing arts and foreign languages, constitutes the mind and spirit of our culture."[44] Under "implementing recommendations" there is nothing about the fine or performing arts, only about the Five New Basics. They do say that the arts "complement the New Basics, and they should demand the same level of performance as the Basics."[45] Peering through the doubletalk, we can see that the Commissioners continue the belief of many educators, taxpayers, and school boards, that the arts are an adjunct only, certainly secondary to the "New Basics." In other words, the report wants schools to be "business as usual" rather than really looking inward, debating, and holding open the possibility of transformation of the schools, students, and society.

It must be concluded that the report from the Commission on Excellence really calls for more of what education presently has: mediocrity. It asks schools, colleges, and universities to adopt more rigorous and measurable standards and higher expectations but proposes no way of funding this changeover. It suggests that "grades should be indicators of academic achievement so they can be relied on as evidence of a student's readiness for further study."[46] This is naive at best. Education should not be an industrial process nor should teachers and students be viewed as pieces of machinery. Motivation comes from a person's desire to do, to want, to have access, to be able to follow wishes. Grades keep most of this from happening, cause students to be competitive in a negative way, and are so subjective that the same essay read by five different teachers would be graded with five different marks. Regarding time, it should be said that if something is not working, longer time devoted to it will usually result in greater frustration, not in better results. More is not necessarily better.

The report closes with a section called "America Can Do It." It states, "The American educational system has responded to previous challenges with remarkable success."[47] It does not say what the previous challenges were, nor what was the "remarkable success." It does mention that "From the late 1800s through the mid-20th century, American schools provided the educated work force needed to seal the success of the Industrial Revolution and to provide the margin of victory in two world wars."[48] Today we know that war is outdated, and the Industrial Revolution is over. If these are the remarkable successes the report speaks about, many would question them at least on moral and ethical grounds, and others would question them on political grounds. Could the Commission members tell us how many Blacks and Hispanics were in the schools from the late 1880s to the mid-20th century? How many people from Appalachia and the inner cities were part of the educated work force of which the Commission speaks? In its scope, the report is narrow, in its facts, the report is selective, passing over with ease such things as slavery, segregation, and present statistics, and failing to show understanding of how children and adults learn. The report is guilty of choosing outdated, warmed over, politically safe ideas, and calling them "challenges." It leaves much to be desired.

3

The Art of Education

Beauty, Leisure, and Allurement

The Golden Age spoken about in Greek and Roman myth refers to an age of personal prosperity, advancement, and cultural achievement. Throughout history, people and movements have spoken of its return, and in our present epoch many are sensing that a New Age may be upon us. José A. Arguelles speaks of it as a transformative vision:

> A rhythm more powerful and inexorable than the rhythm of human reason is sweeping through the human race, a rhythm that springs from deep within the bowels of the earth and resonates with the most distant reaches of stellar space.[1]

And almost two decades ago Ruth Nanda Anshen said:

> We stand at the brink of an age of a world in which human life presses forward to actualize new forms. The false separation of man and nature, of time and space, of freedom and security, is acknowledged, and we are faced with a new vision of man in his organic unity and of history offering a richness and diversity of quality and majesty of scope hitherto unprecedented.[2]

The signs of which Arguelles and Anshen speak are seen throughout the global village. Through an understanding of ecology and environment the split between man and nature is beginning to be healed. Through conferences and dialogues, theologians, scientists, and artists are seeking ways mutually to empower these complementary disciplines. Men are getting in touch with their anima, and women are getting in touch with their animus. The medical profession is speaking in terms of health and holism rather than just sickness. Education is being seen in a more holistic and ongoing way. Nations are beginning to make alliances based more on mutual survival than on the desire for expansion. This may well be an age similar in some ways to the age of the Gothic cathedrals when social forces brought together artisans from all walks of life to participate in building Europe's great cathedrals. This was an age when beauty was relished, when leisure was honored, and people followed their allurements. It is quite probable that the New Age will rest upon these three ancient pillars of wisdom because beauty, leisure, and allurement support us in becoming human.

Education needs to rest on the foundation of this wisdom, or it will have little truth to offer its students. However, it is difficult today for students to be exposed to these ideals for they are in short supply in a quick-fix, fast-food culture. This describes the difficulty we have in trying to live fully in a culture that is proscribed. John Holt names the problem when he says, "Schools cling more and more stubbornly to their mistaken idea that education and teaching are industrial processes, to be designed and planned from above in the minutest detail and then imposed on teachers and their even more passive students."[3] When the truth of beauty, leisure, and allurement is missing from life, our pain is so great that we become addicted to the eternal search to keep busy, thinking we will ultimately find fulfillment among our works or that by buying things our consumer society will heal us. It will not. Without beauty, leisure, and allurement, we will succumb to the inane and the trivial, going deeper into the morass.

Beauty

Beauty, a delight to the senses, can offer a way out of the morass, and it needs to be part of education. It usually is not considered, because we wrongly conceptualize that beauty is a part of progress. Rollo May tells us that "beauty and progress have no relationship at all." He further states "the way to test if something is true is not that it works, but how beautiful it is."⁴ Dealing almost exclusively with the ways things work, schools today miss the larger picture of beauty. Nor would they fare well on May's test, for there is little of beauty about our schools.

Outside of a few art courses, today's educational curriculum does not address our cosmic connections, the deepest dimension of culture. Beauty, leisure, and allurement are all but unheard of, yet these are the elements which give power to a culture. Gene Marine says,

> Culture makes us one, brings us together, is the educational cement that can bind an aging Portuguese-Californian writer to an eager young Nisei playwright, a militant black activist to a cynical white senator, even for an hour. Learning about technology leaves all of us within our own removed groups; learning about Bach or the Modern Jazz Quartet breaks down the cellular membranes of our subcultural privacies.⁵

Although beauty has within itself the power to affect people deeply, and even though it abounds in our world, it is still largely unseen, unfelt by students. Pablo Casals says, "Beauty is all around us, but how many are blind to it! People take little pleasure in the natural and quiet and simple things of life."⁶ Meditating upon the flowering of a tree in spring produces an energy which, through a gentling process, changes a person. Wonder replaces certitude, humility replaces doctrine, microcosm and macrocosm become clearer, understanding and wisdom emerge. The person is more peaceful.

This wisdom was understood by the thirteenth century mystic and theologian Meister Eckhart, who had sound advice to all who would preach and teach: "If I spent enough time with the tiniest creature—even a caterpillar—I would never have to prepare a sermon."⁷ Eckhart, a person in touch with truth, a mystic of Germany's lush and majestic Rhineland, allowed beauty to teach him. Where are our students today who meditate on caterpillars and trees in blossom? What have we done to rob them of their wonderful curiosity? How must we live today, and how must our educational system adjust to allow beauty to teach our students?

Beauty itself will shed a great light upon our questions, offering us a way out of our dilemma. For there is a timelessness in beauty which will put us in touch with the processes of the universe and with our past. It is from our past, from our remembering, that the truth of beauty affects us. The ancient Greeks have written rich treatises on beauty. Dante offers us a vision of it in writing about Beatrice. The universe itself, billions of years young, is a willing teacher. Forests speak their stories to those who seek them out. Oceans tell of power. Storms manifest the cleansing of the atmosphere. Rivers and lakes teem with life, ready to tell us their unique story. Planets and stars want us to know about the combination and recombination of gases. Animals and insects teach us about food chains. Flowers offer us a visual delight which sets our hearts spinning.

The profound mystery of beauty is contemplated when we reach back and wonder, reach back and touch this magnificent universe and turn from ways which violate its magnificence. Not to touch our past, not to remember, is sad indeed. Being a partial participant at life's banquet will always leave us wanting. Our vision will always be distorted and unclear; shapes and forms generalized, never particularized. But there is hope. Dante is still being read. Renoir's paintings are still evoking insight. Tolstoy's ideas are still being debated. The pyramids are still being contemplated. The Aztec sundial is still the basis for our understanding of time. Mozart is still being heard. Chartres Cathedral is still humbling pilgrims. The summer solstice is still being celebrated. The beauty of our universe will teach us about beauty itself, and through patience and humility we will learn. But we must let go of our desires to fill every minute with activity—much of it meaningless—let go so that we can let be, and learn from this great teacher, beauty.

To do this is to admit the larger picture. When the astronauts were circling the earth, they saw all at once the Great Wall of China, the Indian Ocean, the Russian steppes, North and South America, the Atlantic and Pacific Oceans. They, perhaps more than any of us, realize the beauty of our world and what it is to be a citizen of this world. It is time for our educational institutions to admit that from beauty can come this world citizenship. Educators cannot wait for an official government pronouncement. The last thing politicians will admit is that nationalism is dead, that it has not worked well in the past and cannot work now or in the future. Education has to begin teaching *planetism,* for this is the new understanding which beauty offers as a cosmic connection. Nationalism believes it can live with one hundred other nationalisms. It cannot. The Greek culture was destroyed in part because it lost its roots of beauty and could not get past its insistence on city-states. A case could be made that we too have lost our roots of beauty, especially in our barbarism, in dispossessing native Americans, in hacking apart our forests, in humiliating the land with our railroads, and in sabotaging the land with our technology. Fortunately the good which is deep in the native soil cannot be routed out even during centuries of violence. Native peoples and other seekers of truth and peace are still open to telling us their story about beauty if we will but listen. Listening requires that we be people of leisure, that we enter a serenity which springs from the mysterious nature of the universe itself.

Leisure

Many of us define leisure as an absence of work. We think that a day "off" or a trip someplace is leisure. It may be, but probably it is not. Why? Because true leisure is "the art of silence and insight, the ability for non-activity."[8] It is not hectic activities, draining amusements, or sitting in a bar waiting for a drink. It is contemplation of nature and of God. Plato said leisure was a nourishing, feasting, divine celebration of the gods.[9] The psalmist said it similarly: "Have leisure and know that I am God."[10] Joseph Pieper calls leisure "the basis of culture."[11] The relevance of leisure and its importance for education is not difficult to understand. Schools which teach only partial truths produce anemic and starved students. Because of education's dualistic approach, it has disallowed truth while pursuing folly; it has shied away from the connectedness and the holism of the universe. Dick Gregory says: "There isn't a Catholic moon and a Baptist sun. I know the universal God is universal . . . I feel that the same God-force that is the mother and father of the pope is also the mother and father of the loneliest wino on the planet."[12] True education contemplates all creation, including what is said by all bipeds. We cannot rule out something because we choose to label it spiritual. Contemplation and leisure are beyond labels. None of us on the planet, guru, pope, TV evangelist, priest, priestess, or sage, has either all the truth or a monopoly on any part of it. Each of us has the ability to contemplate, to practice leisure, to let it work in and through us to shed another beam of light on the surface of the planet.

Greater than we is the truth of nature and the universe of which we are not only parts, but relative newcomers. We cannot ignore this truth. The practice of leisure, through symbols, myths, seasonal celebrations, and rituals, helps us learn about grandeur, about the immensity of the universe, about its sacred character, about its ways of working. School is a wonderful place to express these sacred rituals, to contemplate various beliefs about our universe, to celebrate festivals. Starhawk speaks about an attitude all of us need to have so that we can reverence the cosmos: "I am not proposing a new belief system, but . . . I am talking about choosing an attitude: choosing to take this living world, the people and creatures on it, as the ultimate meaning and purpose of life, to see the world, the earth, and our lives as sacred."[13] It is leisure which enables us to develop this sacred element.

Education should promote the deep meaning of leisure. That which brings life needs to be a part of school; it helps us understand our cosmic connections and why it is that we are living on the earth. In its rightful context it enhances life. While the Hebrew Bible and the New Testament are debated as possible textbooks, the scripture of the earth, which is far older than any record kept in books by people, has been left untouched and bereft of its transforming power. Students need to know what it is they believe, and how to enlarge their beliefs or change them when that is appropriate to do. They need to view the earth as a living book, a breathing holy of holies, something to both contemplate and participate in. They need a dialogue with leisure to see into the face of wisdom.

Pieper observes that ". . . leisure in Greek is 'skole,' and in Latin 'scola,' the English 'school.' The word used to designate the place where we educate and teach is derived from a word which means 'leisure.' 'School' does not, properly speaking, mean school, but leisure."[14] Subscribing to his definition greatly changes the face of education. School becomes a place where leisure is practiced, a place where the art of silence and insight is manifested, a place where inactivity is honored, a place where, as Thomas Aquinas put it, "we can follow our natural bent in the right way."[15] Following our "natural bent" means that what we do is characterized by effortlessness. Effortlessness is an integral part of leisure.

To practice leisure and effortlessness schools will have to change. They will have to take on the tenor of pre-schools, settings where children learn on their own by assimilating various tasks, including listening, celebrating, using all their senses, the social skills of sharing and getting along with each other. Schools will have to adopt an atmosphere of leisure which treasures creativity and promotes courage. Students, teachers, and administrators need to be enabling, guiding, and creating in a space where soft music fills the air, where freely and playfully they share the wonder of learning.

Although this is the kind of school which makes enormous sense for our children, our nation, and our world, it will not be created easily. Pieper aptly names our predicament: "man seems to mistrust everything that is effortless; he can only enjoy, with a good conscience, what he has acquired with toil and trouble; he refuses to have anything as a gift."[16] The practice of leisure itself can teach students about receiving gifts. It can teach them how to go with the flow of the universe. It can teach them not about being busy, but about letting things happen. In leisure, students enlarge their capacity for steeping themselves in the whole of creation. Nothing is left out, no filters are in place. They will absorb what they can from the total environment in an undistorted and unedited way. They will honor mystery rather than viewing it as a puzzle needing to be solved. With feelings of affirmation students and teachers will enter into a spiral dance celebrating the festival of life. In this celebrating, in holding feasts, in remembering the larger affairs of life, leisure will take hold and we will all begin to experience the world in a different and effortless way.

Allurement

The different and effortless way is the way of allurement. "Allurement" means not only to be attracted and enchanted, but to have a love affair. Imagine students so enchanted with education, with school, that they would have a love affair with it; an "affair of the heart" with school! Allurement would be the modus operandi of our educational institutions and a new worldview would emerge.

This worldview would enable us to envision education in a new way. It would be both the focal point and the backdrop against which courses of study would be organized. Students would discover the great surprise that ideas and people are interesting. Their interest would blossom into fascination, the world of fantasy, and play. They would find school alluring and fascinating. School would be on their minds and in their hearts all of the time. Brian Swimme says: "To become fascinated is to step into a wild love affair on any level of life."[17] He goes on to say that we are not the only life which operates this way, for allurement—having love affairs—is the way of the universe: "We awake to our own unique sets of attractions. So do oxygen atoms. So do protons." He tells us further, "By pursuing your allurements, you help bind the universe together. The unity of the world rests on the pursuit of passion."[18]

Education that fascinates and allures will not only keep students' interest, but will help them direct their passions in harmonious ways with the unity of the universe. It will energize them in their natural flow of curiosity and learning, and they will not feel restricted. This is a deeply profound and humble way of looking at education, for it is the way of the universe itself.

The New "Three R's": Reverence, Renewal, and Responsibility

The "three R's" of our educational system have traditionally referred to "readin', 'ritin', and 'rithmetic." While many of us respond with a smile at this well known and standard curriculum, we know there is much more to education than the "three R's." However, it is to this amusing concept that people usually harken back even when deep educational questions surface. Educators need to pursue a newer and more cosmic dimension of the three R's, one in which reverence, renewal, and responsibility undergird the educational system and develop meaning in learning. For without this more cosmic understanding of the "three R's," there may not be a system of education or even a planet for us to hand on to later generations.

Reverence

"Reverence" is defined as "a feeling or attitude of deep respect, love, and awe, as for something sacred . . ."[19] It refers to the quality of holiness for what is. "What is" means all creation, all that has evolved, all that is interconnected. Matthew Fox says "'what is' may be a child or a dog, a leaf or an ocean, a song or a thought, a painting or a movement, an idea or a dying patient, a birth, a prisoner, or a sunset."[20] Reverence refers to how we *stand* with that "what is": how we act toward it, how our institutions interact with it. "What is," is noble. Because we are creatures of this nobility, we must live and act in a noble way. Reverencing the creation is that noble way.

Reverence is learned in many ways, from letting go, from meditation, from leisure, from contemplating beauty, from following our allurements, from pain, from suffering. Many times people begin to sense the sacredness of life only after the death of a loved one, or after some tragedy has befallen them. But reverence is not only taught through pain and suffering, it can be taught simply by entering fully into all that lives. Robert Muller says:

> We must feel part of all space and time, of the greatness and wonders of the universe . . . . You must . . . know and love your planetary home as well as your universal home, from the infinitely large to the infinitely small. We must stand in awe before the beauty and miracle of creation.[21]

Educators live out their own nobility and impart reverence in the *way* they conduct and teach in their schools. Showing respect to students, making sure that the curriculum is centered in the creation and that teaching methods make sense, and giving up demanding behavior, instills reverence in students. Showing a vision of wholeness, being an encouraging person, taking time with students, making them feel important, and honoring them, recognizing the sacred character of their being, also instills reverence in students.

Reverence is catching. When one person shows respect to another, or to a creature or a rock, an example is given which ignites the tinder of the heart. Feelings of goodness are imparted. Care and concern become evident. Empowerment happens. People of reverence stand in *awe* of "what is"; they recognize its sacredness. They are profoundly concerned with life, with love, and with the pursuit of meaning and harmony in all they do.

Education needs people of reverence to bring out the goodness that is in all students, to validate the creation, and to help create the structures whereby renewal in students and the educational system can take place.

Renewal

"Renewal" means "to make new again; make young, fresh, or strong again."[22] It comes about by making the past into a present which takes on a new vibrancy, thus making it even more alluring. It is, in a sense, what a composer does when reworking the stirrings of music into a new piece. Or what a playwright does when reworking ideas from a book. Teachers and lecturers practice renewal when they take their own ideas and those of others and mold them and present them in such a way that they and their students are "renewed," or "made strong again." It is renewal, presenting ideas, facts, and concepts in such stimulating and new ways, that gets students to think, to ponder, to experiment. This is the building aspect of education; it is what makes the educational process ongoing and creates new learning.

Renewal happens in education when knowledge and ideas are brought together in such a way as to be made fresh. Too many educators present their ideas and the packaging of those ideas in ways that are old and frayed. The ideas and the knowledge become too palatable, too bland. They have no power, no kick. They fail to stimulate, fail to get students to connect. Renewal can help educators revive their ideas by looking at them in different ways, seeing the painting upside down so to speak, and in that new light, seeing something never seen before, or understanding something in a new and imaginative way.

Renewal in education is similar to renovation in a home. That which has always been there gets renewed; changed, updated, streamlined, or embellished, depending on the times. The inheritance becomes new again. Renewal in education means that a teacher does not get out last years' notes and "teach" them to students. Rather, a teacher thinks about the content, plays with it, tries it out in many different configurations, works it and reworks it — much like the potter does with clay — and offers it to eager students in a new and different way. Through this process, both the students and the teacher feel refreshed with content that is made alive, strong, and young again.

Renewal means that teachers are constantly updating their files. They know what is in them, they know how to find ideas, they know how to find the latest magazine article on next week's lesson. Teachers who practice renewal have a wider capacity for thinking and a deeper capacity for feeling. They also make connections more often and more easily. These teachers are more alive and are spurred on by different input from friends and colleagues. Rather than being threatened by the new or variations of the old, they welcome all ideas. They get excited by them. They act on them. In this they feel refreshed and strong. They keep up their enthusiasm, and they are more able to reverence their students because they think less in fixed categories and are more willing to stand in awe. These teachers usually look for a more unusual way of making their presentations. Not satisfied with talking about certain facts, they want their students to *experience* the facts. This might mean visiting a forest, which will speak to students and teach them lessons in wonder; holding a ritual by a lake or an ocean, which will enable students to commune directly with the beauty of nature; spending time with painters, poets, and musicians. Rather than reading about how air is pumped into a tunnel, teachers who practice renewal take their class behind the scene at a local tunnel. Or barring a local tunnel, they visit a shop which sells air compressors and arrange a demonstration. Or they get a film on the building of subways, or the building of the St. Louis Arch, or they get a miner to talk about air and breathing in a mine. Failing all this, teachers who renew make arrangements with a prison to talk with a prisoner who spent a night in an air vent trying to escape.

Renewal puts a wonderful face on education. It makes it come alive, it makes learning in school exciting. After all, schools can frequently do what individuals cannot. A prison warden may not want individual students coming to the prison at different times, but would be more than happy to welcome a class that could spend a few hours. Furthermore, there can be more group interaction when the whole class participates in such an outing; and the chances for wider and more exciting learning are increased. Finally, renewal leads to the desire to change structures, to make justice happen in the world. Our schools need to invest heavily in the power of renewal, and then share this fruit with churches, synagogues, business, and communities. For renewal creates the ability to see things differently, and it ultimately brings hope.

Responsibility

"Responsibility" is defined as "a condition of being responsible," that is, a personal accountability, obligation, dependability, or duty,[23] to persons and the world, and by extension even to the universe itself. In its broad context it means also teaching justice and modelling justice in the world. Responsibility means both holding accountable and responding, being in charge of oneself and going out to others, and acting on those deep feelings and events which concern each of us and our planet. "Responsibility," says Matthew Fox, "means birthing, with others, a community of caring, celebrative, reverent persons who can feel and be honest with one another."[24] For educators, responsibility means being willing continually to undergo the birthing process in themselves and with all of their students. It means "staying with" students in good times and in bad, and looking again and again at a way to get through. Responsible educators have a great amount of personal power. They do not "give up" nor do they have unrealistic expectations either of themselves or their students. Because they are responsible, they work with their students in giving birth to reverence, care, and justice in the whole of creation.

There is a cosmic dimension which responsible education must address. It must speak of the universal forces and interconnections within all of creation. It must also speak of, and to, the spiritual dimension of created beings. It must recognize our cosmic connections during these past twenty billion years and seek to make us more aware of how this interconnectedness works. Einstein alluded to education's role in responsibility to our cosmic dimension when he said: "The most important function of art and science is to awaken the cosmic religious feeling and keep it alive."[25] This cosmic dimension must never be allowed to be eclipsed. Harmony, beauty, interdependence, and all the other components of the natural world are kept at bay when our systems

THE ART OF EDUCATION

of education isolate students from nature and the rest of the real and natural world. Mary Caroline Richards reminds us:

> Our planet is our school, and far beyond:
> our church, our shop and study, and our fields.
> We are all learning to awake:
> awake in dream, in meditation and in prayer.
> Inspired awake!
> Inspired awake!
> We feel it thus: one mighty school,
>   the teaching everywhere.[26]

The native peoples of America have echoed this. They have always perceived themselves as part of the larger whole, part of the coasts, the woodlands, the deserts, always an integral part of creation. "Mother earth," "grandmother moon," "grandfather wind," was how these people discerned. All the elements of the universe were elements of their lives. All the happenings of the cosmos were happenings that impinged upon them. No rain would visit their land that would come unnoticed or be thought unneeded. Indeed rain is seen as a cleansing ritual for the atmosphere. What high school student today has this kind of reverence for rain? Alas, for most of us, rain is something we are usually dissatisfied with save for when it is necessary for the farmers and our lawns. When rain comes we usually judge that it is too much, or too fierce, or too little, or it has ruined some plans we had to go to the beach.

How out of touch we have become — if we moderns ever were in touch — with our cosmos and its functions and our responsibility to it. Naming the forces of nature, the powers of the earth, the potencies and potentialities is commonplace and necessary for our red brothers and sisters; a people among whom disease was almost unheard of until the white man came; a people who trust, a people who care and understand what it is to reverence. Frederick Turner was unfortunately correct when he said:

> Every added protection against the natural world contributes its bit to the steadily building illusion of independence from nature, so that in time that greatest of illusions is erected: the omnipotence of man.[27]

We need to face the fact that Turner's prophetic voice is correct. The omnipotence of man is here, already upon us making chaos

TRANSFORMING EDUCATION

out of beauty. Education must have some share in this irresponsibility.

Is it too late to make a change? No. It is not too late to reaffirm the cosmos as the power, not too late to find our rightful place within the cosmos. It is not too late for education to become prophetic, to plan, to be responsible. But when we gather to plan, the universe needs to be there. When we look out over these next hundred years, the universe needs to be there. When we make decisions on how to stop our pollution, how to live in harmony with nature, how to abide with all the created species, the universe needs to be there. When we gather around us all the folks who inhabit the land and determine policies for ourselves, the universe needs to be there. Brian Swimme puts the argument well in his penetrating look at the universe:

> To begin to evaluate the achievement of the humans, we might take a democratic vote. Let's not be chauvinistic here—let "everyone" vote. There are 10 million species presently alive on the planet. Convene the United Species Conference, giving each species one vote, and put this question to the test: "Should the human species be allowed to remain within the Earth's system of life?" Imagine the debate. Our single representative would attempt to persuade 9,999,999 others that the human species is indeed worth keeping.[28]

The universe needs to be present in our thoughts, our planning, and it needs to be present in our schools. After twelve years of compulsory education students cannot identify with the universe itself; this is a sad fact. Most high school graduates have little or no idea where our oxygen comes from, know little or nothing about the fragility of the atmosphere, the need for electrical storms, or the saving work of the prokaryotes more than three billion years ago. When we cannot identify with the universe, is it any wonder that we become so prone to destroy it? Thomas Berry says that,

> If we were truly moved by the beauty of the world about us we would honor the earth in a profound way. We would understand immediately and turn away with a certain horror from those activities that violate the integrity of the planet.[29]

The time is now for the citizens of the globe to develop educational systems which engender reverence and gratitude for these wonders. Matthew Fox says that every person is capable of (loving) the universe but most people are not encouraged to find their relationship with it and celebrate it. He asks: "Then what happens to persons and their institutions? They become sick and violent. For we were made for something cosmic and will not fit peacefully into anything much smaller."[30] Andrew Weil puts it this way: "the universe is a conspiracy organized for my benefit."[31]

It behooves us to be responsible and design a curriculum that ensures our students develop the capabilities to understand and love passionately this self-organizing celestial sphere. "We need a curriculum that will help develop a new language," says Thomas Berry, "one that is primarily a language of the earth, of living relationships that extend throughout the universe."[32] How wonderful it would be to picture all our citizens loving the earth enough to view it in reverent respect, a profound sense of esteem, as each bends the knee in honor of that which gave each of us life.

Our educational system needs to allow the universe to present itself, its inner workings, and the goings on of its outer space. It needs to trumpet the facts that the universe is always a winner, that it has been efficiently working for twenty billion years, that it works in *both* novelty and confirmation, without waste and without fatigue.

Study of the universe, its dynamics, and interconnections can unfold wonderfully in our schools. We certainly have the time. Under mandatory education laws, our children are in school for a minimum of twelve years. Most schools usually run thirty-six to thirty-eight weeks, a minimum of one hundred eighty days per year, or 2,160 days over the twelve years. Imagine if students learned one new technique in caring for the universe for each of the weeks they were in school. When they entered young adulthood, college, work, or took a year off, they would have at their fingertips over four hundred and thirty-two techniques for caring for their environment. For the first time in a century our ground water could have a chance to begin the long, arduous process of cleansing itself from the chemicals of pesticides. Our air and atmosphere might begin to recover from the daily deployment of pollutants from industry which would have learned to care. The cells of all living organisms could begin to breathe a sigh of relief as cancer in all its forms begins its slide from dominancy. The land of this planet could once again bring forth species, scents, and fragrances unheard of in modern times but fully known before settlers and reigning technocracy brought destruction and acid rain. Instead of trying to alter the DNA of an organism we would strive to re-purify our environment so that the DNA would replicate the way it has until the modern period: accurately and healthily.

Imagine if students learned one new way to care about themselves each week they were in school.

Would the drug situation of today still exist?

Would compulsive eating and dieting be necessary?

Would tobacco be a problem?

Would alcohol be endemic and epidemic?

Would families have more positive interactions?

Would the sham rites of passage: cars, credit cards, sexual exploitation, smoking, drinking, and other put-downs be acceptable?

Would pushing, shoving, and hitting, still be the norm of behavior on the playground?

Would the arms of war still be our country's highest technological export?

Imagine if students learned one new form of art every twelve weeks during this time. By the time they were young adults they would have been exposed to thirty-six art forms! Imagine their choices for careers when they have been enlightened by thirty-six art forms.

How many potters have we lost because of our dualistic educational system?

How many possible artists have we sent to jail because we gave them no means of artistic expression when we mandated that they spend all this time in our institutions of learning and higher learning?

How many sculptors have gone undeveloped?

How many opportunities to dramatize a difficult situation and thereby empower both students and adults to have honest dialogue have been lost because our educational systems have failed to draw out the artist in everyone?

THE ART OF EDUCATION

> How many poets have we consigned to the humdrum of daily existence because we never bothered to allow them to express their deeper inspirations?
>
> How many dancers have we kept down, how many musicians, how many mimes and storytellers, how many potential film makers, how many puppeteers and jugglers—in how many photographers, jazz pianists, cake decorators, and cooks, have we doused the spark of initiative?

Imagine if students learned the beauties, the subtleties, the pride and the passion of one culture per semester in all the years they spent in school. By the time our students graduated high school they would have been exposed to twenty-four different cultures who reside in this, our global village. Twenty-four different expressions of what it is to be human, of what it is to love, to care, to share. How different would this country be if our students learned not only to know about, but to know perhaps very deeply, children, women, and men of other cultures? When these, our children, become adults and get into agriculture, industry, business, leisure, travel, computers, real estate, building, manufacturing, education, foreign service, government, medicine, counseling, painting, pottery, photography, and poetry; how might their view of the world be different? We could not begin to count the ways. Perhaps the need to exploit would be lessened because our children would not only know about the culture they were dealing with, but would be friends with the very people who represented that culture.

Students who had been exposed to many different cultures, who had spent summers and winters and become friends with those of another land would become tomorrow's government officials. One wonders how quickly they would create policies which export war to those with whom they share real friendship and love.

> Would they engage in the shortsighted policies and agendas of quota systems to justify raising prices on the home front?
>
> Would they not spend time in ethical planning for the good of the whole planet?
>
> Would not the "them" and "us" mentality of so many of our present world leaders shrink into oblivion?
>
> Would present policies of apartheid be tolerated?

TRANSFORMING EDUCATION

Would Bhopal and Chernobyl have happened?

It is so difficult to kill, either through bullets or policies, those with whom we have shared a cosmic vision and responsibility for the earth, those with whom we have really been intimate.

What would happen to students exposed to the art, music and languages of these twenty-four different cultures? Imagine learning about the Falkland Islands, Grenada, Lebanon, Israel, Nicaragua, Viet Nam, Chile, Mexico, and other great nations on the globe by getting to know them through their music, their art, their science, their engineering, their food, their dance, their medicine, their schools, and their poetry. What a delight to have our students singing the songs of Albania, wearing the clothing of Turkey, cooking the food of Hungary, reading the poetry of Russia, preparing the tea of England, sculpting the shrines of Botswana, playing the music of Peru, reciting the playlines of the Zimbabwe stage, choreographing the folk dances of the Mediterranean! Can you see the joy on the faces of students coming home from schools which really understood what the cosmic dimension of education is all about? Students would be happy to know more about their friends on the other side of the world. Students would care enough to learn the rudiments of others' languages. Could we as a nation begin to learn from our students and be brought in part by them into a wonderful, workable, desirable future?

When the "three R's" of reverence, renewal, and responsibility become the foundation of our educational system, our educational system will change for the better. As long as these ideals are missing, or only given lip service, education will evoke neither the innate goodness of students nor the moral learning society needs to deal ethically with its own members and people of other cultures. Thomas Berry says we must speak about values, about how things came to be, how they came to be as they are, and how the future life of human beings can be given some satisfying direction.[33] Educators can no longer afford to miss this larger picture. Some people may bristle at the need for values to be discussed in school, sensing that only certain values would be taught. To bristle at this is to miss what education really is about. Gregory Bateson reminds us that wisdom is the intelligence of the system as a whole.[34] Reverence, renewal, and responsibility will help us construct our new human story so that we can value and live in harmony with the whole which is all creation.

4

Forgotten Values in Education

The new educational system must be based on a firm psychological foundation, with nurturance as the footing. Nothing less will work. Nothing less will help students develop meaning in their lives. Nurturance is the nourishment, the food which supplies the nutrients human beings need to grow, to mature, to become whole. Without nurturance, human beings will atrophy; they will be insufficient; they will fail to reach their potential. In this chapter nurturance will be viewed within a framework of acceptance, touch, and trust; of admiration and encouragement; of wonder, play; creativity, and celebration; and of choices and consequences.

Acceptance, Touch, and Trust

Acceptance, touch, and trust are some of the first manifestations of nurturance in our lives. They are part of the initial qualities which need to be offered to us from birth; they are certainly as important as eating. In a sense, they should have been present to us psychically from the moment of conception. Once a couple finds out they are pregnant, the acceptance, touch, and trust they have for each other becomes shared with their fetus. These qualities of nurturance need to be with us throughout all of our lives. In healthy people they become the basis of all meaningful interactions.

TRANSFORMING EDUCATION

Acceptance

Nurturing can only happen when one person accepts another, for acceptance releases the power in all of us to nurture. Without acceptance, one's ability to nurture will be diminished. If another person must behave a certain way, must look or dress a certain way, must speak a certain way before I can accept him or her, then nurturance will be difficult. For nurturance to happen I must be able consistently to receive that person favorably.

In school there is almost a conspiracy against accepting students as they are. The culprit in all of this? Quite simply it is a combination of personal expectations and the sometimes overwhelming desires educators have for their own acceptance. When nourishment and validation are not forthcoming from their profession, educators frequently turn their unmet needs into unrealistic expectations and transfer them to students and classes. Succumbing to these pressures leaves devastating scars on their students. Leroy Baruth and Daniel Eckstein point out that meeting the challenge of helping to provide for positive experiences in school "often becomes difficult because our present social and educational systems seem to create an environment that sometimes leads to discouragement for the child."[1] Accepting students as they are does not mean having to put up with behavior that is clearly out of order. It does mean that educators have to see the worth of students and create environments in which this worth can be cherished and expanded.

Educators can be more accepting of students' ways and time clocks if they are more accepting of their own. One way of celebrating acceptance is to celebrate errors. This keeps teachers off pedestals and helps develop the courage to be imperfect. Educators need to be able to say, "I made a mistake. I really goofed on that, but I learned so much from it that I'm glad it happened."

Accepting students as they are is perhaps the greatest gift that a teacher can offer. Not based on grades, how they dress, or other arbitrary measures, students can feel in their bones that they belong. In this atmosphere, alienation is hard to take root, loneliness will more often be missing, and the desire to participate, to cooperate with others, and to behave appropriately, will be high.

FORGOTTEN VALUES IN EDUCATION

In *To a Dancing God,* Sam Keen has an enriching chapter entitled "Education For Serendipity," in which he speaks about the need for relationships if people are to grow and mature. He notes also that much in the temperament of modern Americans militates against building relationships, for the average family moves every five years. Because we are so mobile, we tend to try to manufacture relationships or produce them on short notice. Keen says:

> Five years . . . is seeding time for friendship. More time yet is required for the trust and fidelity which make for easy acceptance to ripen. Roots must intertwine, time be wasted together, crises weathered, celebrations shared before the relationship reaches maturity.[2]

Keen's words speak loudly to one of the most crucial areas of modern education: the lack of relationship between teachers and students. In many schools, particularly in large cities, there is little positive and friendly interaction between these two groups. It is not uncommon for teachers in junior high and high school to have "related" with 150 or more students on any given day. In these schools what matters is not relationship but that the curriculum be "taught." There has been little or no bond created, no mentorship established; many times there is no teacher-adult to emulate.

Smaller classes alone will not make a difference in education. Students have to apprentice themselves with a single teacher or with a few teachers or co-teachers, each of whom desires to relate with the other in an ongoing way for at least the "seeding-time" of five years that Keen talks about. One of the strongest links in Rudolf Steiner Education is the Waldorf School's insistence that children be with the same teacher for many years, where possible for eight years.[3] This number of years may not be workable in public schools, but there is a wisdom here that the American public schools can learn from the very remarkable Waldorf system of education. It is the wisdom of full acceptance of all students and the treasure of deep relationships between and among human beings.

Accepting children means loving them and dealing lovingly with them. Concretely, it means aiding them in the development of their strengths, enabling them to deal with their weaknesses, showing them how to redirect the negative into that which has positive gain, and trusting them. Accepting children means to teach them ways of understanding, ways of self-acceptance, ways of change. It means teaching children how to be nurturers themselves and how to be self-nurturers. It means developing an education which accepts, which fosters cooperation, interdependence, freedom, responsibility, consequences for behavior and actions; an education which aids in building character, developing values, and determining beliefs. Some would like education to be value-free and beliefs to be proscribed, but that is not possible. We obviously live out of a value system and our educational system reflects this. It is the job of educators to make sure they provide an environment worthy of imitation.

Robert J. Keeshan, who for twenty-five years was Captain Kangaroo on TV, speaks of the importance of teachers being nurturers: "No question, we are able to dazzle, but all that dazzle is no match for BEING THERE. The teacher is a real life human being, able to address the needs and desires of a specific child. There is a magic all around the classroom. It is an ancient magic — and pity the teacher unaware of those powers."[4] Keeshan's words are especially poignant. There never will be a match for "being there," for the relationship between teachers and students, and for the mutual respect which flows from that relationship. There is a magic in each person, a mystery which each of us gets invited into anew as relationships grow and mature.

Acceptance is not dazzle, but listening, hearing, addressing the desires of a specific child at a particular moment; being "tuned in" to another human being. These things can only be done through warm, human contact. A tape on a machine can get us to laugh, but no machine can understand how we feel at this moment, nor can a machine comfort us when our pet frog dies, our parents fight or separate, or some other major mishap occurs. In these instances we need someone who is "there," someone who can be with us in such a way that we feel it. When we cannot feel it or if our being with others is negative, when we desire acceptance and get put down, we begin emotionally to wither, shrivel up, and atrophy.

In our fast-paced society some adults may not always realize the benefits of listening and being there at just the right moment, but there are many who do. Teachers and other adults need to understand how acceptance is at the same time both a preventative of negative behavior and an exercise in positive behavior.

Teachers show acceptance by making sure their students feel included, by offering them a role in decision-making, by letting them decide the pace they wish to learn something, or whether they wish to learn it at all, and by letting them take the consequences of that action. Teachers show acceptance by letting students help decide what the physical arrangements of the classroom will be, deciding what classroom- and hall-bulletin boards say, what celebrations and decorations they want for Christmas, Hanukah, Chinese New Year, solstice, and other festive occasions, what kind of projects to take on, what committees will be necessary to meet group goals, what the seating arrangements need to be for optimal learning. "Learning to make decisions is an important part of education, a vital preparation for adulthood," says Don Dinkmeyer, Sr., Don Dinkmeyer, Jr., and Gary McKay.[5] Teachers who are accepting recognize this and enjoy the fun of being part of their students' growth and development.

Human beings are social and want to belong, hence, students want to belong also. They want to feel significant, they want to learn. But most of all, they want to have the freedom to "be," to search, to experience joys and triumphs, to learn from mistakes—in short, to act responsibly in their freedom. They need a proper foundation to be able to do this well. Acceptance is part of that foundation. Without acceptance in our schools and homes, students will seek to belong in negative ways, in gangs or mobs. Significance will be sought by having guns, knives, and other weapons. Without acceptance, belonging will be a negative experience and learning will be of a kind that does not teach values but isolates and alienates. Schools need to be places where the power of acceptance happens—being able to touch very deeply the lives of students and their parents and families—and where the magic and mystery of being human unfolds.

Touch

Nurturance first happens to each of us when we are touched. If there is today one area of agreement among the medical, teaching, nursing, and educational professions, it is this: people need touch. Our very life depends upon it. Baby or grandparent, rich or poor, male or female, all races of people hunger for meaningful touch. Education ought not to be fearful of this. When touch is part of students' daily life and activities, students and teachers

TRANSFORMING EDUCATION

alike, gain. Jean Liedloff speaks not only of our need, but of our deprivation and therefore our longing for touch:

> The vast reservoir of longing for physical comforting might be significantly reduced if it became socially acceptable to hold hands with a walking companion of either sex, to sit touching, not just near, talking companions, to sit on people's laps in public as well as in private, to stroke a tempting head of hair when the mood takes one, to hug more freely and more publicly, and in general not to curb one's affectionate impulses unless they would be unwelcome.[6]

Many educators will have great difficulty with what Liedloff proposes. However, the difficulty serves to point out the deep distress we are already in because of our touch deprivation. Reflect on the problems we have in society and schools because of a lack of touch: shyness, fighting, negative sexual experiences, pregnancy in junior high and high schools, venereal disease, misunderstanding, sexual harassment, and a multi-billion dollar a year pornography industry. Obviously, meaningful touch is necessary, and it can easily become a part of everyday school by having teachers introduce it through ritual. Those that introduce touch through ritual will find that students come early to school. Classes where touching is part of being together will be classes with less discipline problems. Classes that teach serious massage will have students lined up waiting to get into them. Nor will these benefits accrue just to students; there will be a tremendous difference among faculty and staff too. It will be common to find teachers happier about their jobs, common to find administrators, teachers and parents viewing each other as equals rather than in a pecking order, because touch breaks through the barriers that keep human beings from expressing their humanness. This is especially important for junior high and high school kids whose form of touching frequently falls between hitting and going to bed with each other, because they have not been taught any avenue for positive nonsexual touch.

When I have used massage in workshops and classes among both students and teachers and a sprinkling of administrators, the results have been consistently the same. The questions begin: "Why can't we have more of this?" "Why can't we have this as part of our curriculum?" Invariably someone asks, "Wouldn't it be great if Congress would begin its deliberations each day with a back rub?" On a family camping weekend with over one hundred children and single parents, massage went on for more than three hours, always with at least one member of the family being massaged by the other family members. The sleeping rooms were distinctly different that night from what they had been on the first night when pandemonium seemed to prevail.

When they are touched in meaningful ways both children and adults change. They become more open, friendlier, more caring, more loving. It is as if someone gave them a transfusion of goodness. Even those experiencing problems and difficulties change very quickly when they are meaningfully touched or touch others. A teenager acting in the most hostile ways usually succumbs to meaningful human touch. An adult who feels out of sorts, even depressed, responds to touch.

We need to put touch in the classrooms across America. From there it will be brought home to the living rooms of America and begin the necessary revolution to greater humanness. It is not enough just to talk about it. It is time to do it. I recall being at a teacher training day where the instructor talked about touch. On and on she went about how important it was to have touch. She related how a librarian could touch a student, how principals could use touch meaningfully, what teachers could do in the classroom. But throughout six hours of the workshop she never once had any of us touch! Obviously we need to have many days of in-service for educators who feel awkward about touching. Because they are human, they can awaken that area of need and response in themselves and ultimately find a comfortable level of touch. Many school districts have retreat-type days before the fall semester begins, and all schools have in-service days. The moaning and groaning that accompanies much of this time will all but disappear once meaningful touch is accepted. Every time I finish a teacher training session using a back rub or a temple massage, I usually get hired for the next training day right there on the spot. Those educators wisely know that touch is an important part of transformation and that it helps build trust.

Trust

When students trust each other with a temple massage, it becomes easier to trust in other areas. It helps them risk expansion: expansion of their mind, their heart, their body, and expansion of relationships. They become more alive, able to ask searching questions, able to speculate, and unafraid to examine, dispute, or challenge. They know they will be accepted and not disapproved or belittled. Put students in an atmosphere of trust and they begin trusting. Put students who have not been trusted before in this environment, and after a few initial tries at mistrust, they too begin trusting. Turn these students loose in a school system, in their homes, in their community, in their churches or synagogues, and look out. Trusting human beings are a power to be reckoned with. What is more, students who trust learn more easily and are more willing to help others. Don Dinkmeyer, Sr., Don Dinkmeyer, Jr., and Gary McKay say:

> The time you spend learning to promote students' social and psychological growth can have a dramatic impact on students' willingness and readiness to learn. Students who feel safe and comfortable in their group — your class — aren't likely to misbehave.[7]

Trust is both caught and taught. It is caught through experiencing it and by example. Teachers who show unconditional acceptance towards their students, who preside over classrooms where mutual respect and empathy are practiced, establish the conditions for trust to be caught. When teachers interact with students in a similar way in which they would interact with their own adult best friends, trust is taught and caught. Rare would be the adult who would yell at his or her best friend, or give orders, or tell them that a work they were completing was not worthwhile. Yet without realizing it, parents and teachers speak to children in these ways. At homes and schools across the country, children daily are yelled at, given orders, and told in other ways that they and their work are not worthwhile. Parents and teachers may not mean to do this, but because patriarchy is so deeply embedded in present family and educational systems, authoritarianism is fostered, and teachers and parents fall into it. A system changes when individuals within that system change. In a trusting classroom students feel free to express themselves totally. Often, teachers like the positive expressions their students exhibit but rarely allow negative expressions. Why? Because we view school and the classroom as a paradigm of learning, by which we mean, authority. "Speak when you're spoken to and be silent the rest of the time." Carl Rogers says that new teachers are often advised:

"Make sure you get control of your students the very first day." He goes on:

> *Trust is at a minimum.* Most notable is the teacher's distrust of the student. The student cannot be expected to work satisfactorily without the teacher constantly supervising and checking on him . . . . Mutual trust is not a noticeable ingredient.[8]

When students are trusted, when they can ventilate their feelings, when they can talk about painful emotions, anger and sadness decrease. When one student feels shy and hears another student open up, or even blast off, the shy student experiences the possibility of a new future. Students know they can "be themselves" in this teacher's classroom.

An excellent way for teachers to show trust in students is by encouraging them to become peer facilitators in which they learn communication skills and use them with other students in lower grades. They usually visit these grades once a week and have classroom discussion and followup with their own teachers and fellow students. This very successful program used in many schools reports students having a great deal more self-esteem, becoming more trusting and better listeners. Tom Erney and Robert D. Myrick talk about peer facilitators:

> A peer facilitator is someone who cares about others and who talks with them about their thoughts and feelings. Rather than being an "advice-giver," or "problem-solver," a peer facilitator is a sensitive listener who uses communication skills to encourage self-exploration and decision-making.[9]

In addition to "peer" meaning "an equal," it is an acronym from "*P*ositive *E*ducational *E*xperiences in *R*elationships,"[10] which focuses on strengths and potentials of young people. Through a peer program students learn to trust not only themselves and one another, but their teachers and their administrators. PEER has a tremendous effect on these latter groups also. As teachers and administrators begin trusting each other, traditional administrator-teacher power blocks dissolve. Goethe perceived well the implications of self-trust and other-trust when he wrote, "If you treat a person as if he already were what he potentially could be, you make him what he should be." It is only through trust that we learn about life, love, ecstasy, and our place within the universe.

An educational system based on trust, based on seeing the potential as if it already exists, becomes a spawning ground for human growth.

Admiration and Encouragement

After the foundation of nurturance is built through acceptance, touch, and trust, the building up of the student's personality structure continues with the addition of admiration and encouragement. Both are extremely important. It is an unfortunate fact that today there is little of either of these ingredients in the public schools. Educators who have allowed themselves to be more involved with test scores and less involved with admiration and encouragement need to realize that the result of their efforts is frequently a negative payoff in students. Students who have not been admired and encouraged experience personal difficulties and a lack of feeling worthwhile; they lack esteem deep inside themselves.

Admiration

"Admiration" means to regard with delight and pleased approval; to hold in high regard. Years ago it meant to marvel at. Educators who are nurturers admire. They admire themselves, their students, their colleagues; they admire life and creation, they admire their professions.

All human beings are lovable and capable.[11] But to comprehend fully the depth and breadth of our lovableness and capabilities, we need to be admired, need to be affirmed, need to be marveled at and accepted. What a change comes into the classrooms of America when students and teachers marvel at each other, when they are delighted by each other, when the whole school population is caught up just in the presence of each other. When this does not go on, when educational systems and teachers get caught up in their collective syllabus and disregard admiration, the effect can be deadly. Witness what Naomi White wrote in the November, 1943, issue of *Progressive Education:*

> I have taught in high school for ten years. During that time I
> have given assignments, among others, to a murderer, a pugilist,
> a thief and an imbecile. The murderer was a quiet little boy who
> sat on the front seat and regarded me with pale blue eyes; the
> pugilist lounged by the window and let loose at intervals in a
> raucous laugh that startled even the geraniums; the thief was a
> gay-hearted Lothario with a song on his lips; and the imbecile, a
> shifty-eyed little animal seeking the shadows.
>
> The murderer awaits death in the state penitentiary; the
> pugilist lost an eye in a brawl in Hong Kong; the thief, by standing
> on tip-toe, can see the window of my room from the county
> jail; and the once gentle-eyed little moron beats his head against
> a padded wall in the state asylum.
>
> All these pupils once sat in my room, sat and looked at me
> gravely across worn brown desks. I must have been a great help
> to those pupils . . . . I taught them the rhyming scheme of the
> Elizabethan sonnet and how to diagram a complex sentence.[12]

Although written over forty years ago, there is still unfortunately a loud ring of truth to this very clear piece of writing. Oh, we have made changes in these past forty years; most educational systems no longer allow our children to be called animals, morons, and imbeciles. Vastly different and improved mental health centers have all but replaced state asylums; today's students would probably not know or care to know what a "gay-hearted Lothario" was, especially since the word gay has a whole new meaning among us. Many students and most teachers, save those who were tracked in literature, would not have the foggiest idea of the rhyming scheme of the Elizabethan sonnet. But this is not the guts of the matter. What is much deeper in the small essay are the questions and attitudes that this teacher is raising. Her last sentences sum up the feelings of one who has had to come to grips with a system that has perpetuated the spurious and called it education.

Pablo Casals says we have to teach our children that they are marvels. He asks,

> When will we teach our children in school what they are? We
> should say to each of them: Do you know what you are? You are
> a marvel. You are unique. In all the world there is no other child
> exactly like you. In the millions of years that have passed there
> has never been another child like you.[13]

Unless teachers can admire, accept, and be delighted in the person of the student, real education cannot take place. Students will still be taught and they will learn, but they will forever lose the development of personality and personhood, of values and self-concepts of worth, competence, responsibility, and importance to society. Students who are not cherished, not looked upon in human ways, and not encouraged, turn into adults and parents who believe they cannot cherish, cannot encourage, cannot act in human ways.

Listen to young adults today. Listen anywhere in the country, North, East, South or West; listen in offices, in movie theatre lines, in restaurants, on the street, in hospitals, in churches. Listen for the admiration of others in their words, in their faces, in their body language. What is all too often heard, seen, and intuited is the put-down. We continue to raise great numbers of people who think ill of themselves and therefore ill of others. There is a fundamental sense of powerlessness among the majority of our citizenry. We have all been deprived, not only in infancy but throughout much of life, of acceptance as a person. Jean Liedloff states that the deprivation is not hopeless, ". . . the experiences missed during the time when the infant ought to have been in-arms could also be supplied later in life, if the means were found to do so."[14] Teachers who admire can be one of those means. They can have a tremendous effect on these low esteem students. Through their admiration, acceptance, and encouragement, they become helpful aids to change their students' beliefs and behavior.

Encouragement

Encouragement stimulates courage, it deals with the heart, the desire to do things on one's own, to be self-motivated. It prepares students for self-sufficiency. Rudolf Dreikurs said:

> . . . teachers have a responsibility that goes beyond imparting facts and teaching skills. There is an even greater responsibility to reach each child and help him find a place in the group where he can find satisfaction and acceptance as a human being, regardless of how well or poorly he performs scholastically.[15]

When a child has not been reached, when a child is greatly discouraged and gives up, he or she is set up for failure. Donald E.

FORGOTTEN VALUES IN EDUCATION

Hamachek says: "It is not the people who feel that they are liked and wanted and acceptable and able who fill our prisons and mental hospitals. Rather, it is those who feel deeply inadequate, unliked, unwanted, unacceptable, and unable."[16] Rudolf Dreikurs says further that "each child needs continuous encouragement just as a plant needs water. He cannot grow and develop and gain a sense of belonging without encouragement."[17] He points out that:

> Half the job of encouraging a child lies in avoiding discouragement either by humiliation or by overprotection. Anything we do that supports a child's lack of faith in himself is discouraging. The other half lies in knowing how to encourage. Whenever we act to support the child in a courageous and confident self-concept, we offer encouragement.[18]

We have so many ways of building our bodies and our minds, but what of our hearts? Encouragement is the process which helps us to focus on strengths and assets and to see possibilities for progress even in the most difficult situations. It is the process of strengthening our hearts. When teachers are encouraging, students feel ten feet tall. It becomes a joy to be in school and a joy to be associated with adults who give confidence in their words, in their looks. Why do students who are encouraged do so well, think so critically, care so much? Because students who are encouraged do not spend much time looking for acceptance or questioning their abilities. Not only do these students believe in themselves, but they realize that others believe in them also. In a sense they become higher achievers because the relationship they have with these adults, their teachers, is meaningful to them. They do not want to risk disappointment, because they care about these people. Imagine what would happen in our schools if encouragement were part of the daily operation. Imagine the changes in families if these students were to bring encouragement into homes across the nation. Imagine what our government would become when students who were continuously encouraged for all their years of education, take their positions as its leaders. Imagine what worker benefits would be like in a large corporation when encouragers sit on its board of directors. How would nursing mothers be looked upon? What kind of child care would the large corporations provide? What kind of ideas would emanate from the minds of top management which took turns overseeing the children of all their employees in the courtyard-playgrounds of the Fortune Five

Hundred?[19] We would come much closer to a global understanding and acceptance of each other. Most important, we would be desirous of mutual cooperation, for that is what encouragement engenders.

In a humorous article entitled "Love and the Cabbie," Art Buchwald relates how he and his friend were riding in a cab in New York when at the end of their taxi ride his friend told the driver: "Thank you for the ride. You did a superb job of driving." Buchwald writes that the driver was stunned for a second, then said, "Are you a wise guy or something?" The friend replied, "No, my dear man, and I'm not putting you on. I admire the way you keep your cool in heavy traffic." Buchwald goes on at length about his friend being some kind of a nut, but his friend prevails in showing forth his unique point of view. It seems the friend believes that he made the driver's day. Furthermore, he believes the driver will be nice to his other fares because someone was nice to him. "Eventually the goodwill could spread to at least 1,000 people."[20] Although it may seem farfetched, this is how the encouragement process works. We can be sure of at least one thing from this piece by Buchwald: there's no doubt that the cabbie would have spoken to his friends, to his colleagues, and perhaps to his wife about this unique fare that rode in his cab. Encouragement is catching.

Another important part of the encouragement process is that it helps the learner develop the courage to be *imperfect.* This was one of the main tenets in Alfred Adler's school of psychology. He wisely recognized the frustration each of us would have if we tried to live our lives perfectly. Yet perfectionism is what many educational institutions desire in their administrators, their teachers, and their students. It is seen over and over again in the pressure for grades, the pressure for winning, the pressures in tryouts for cheerleading and writing for the school newspaper. Robert J. Keeshan says:

> In today's America, the pressure to compete is intense. A child is born and his uncle is already talking about Harvard. There is the ever-present fear of failure from pre-school days on. A child is a late bloomer and is unable to read well at seven — he comments, "I guess I'm a flop in life."[21]

And Urie Bronfenbrenner says:

FORGOTTEN VALUES IN EDUCATION

> Schools have become one of the most potent breeding grounds of alienation in American society. For this reason it is of crucial importance for the welfare and development of school-age children that schools be reintegrated into the life of the community.[22]

One just cannot be perfect. Perfectionism is a negative myth and it needs to be expunged from the record of humanity. Ulcers, some forms of cancer, high blood pressure, all forms of distress, pain, needless suffering, and calamity can result from our love affair with perfectionism. When students have the courage to be imperfect — and it takes a lot of courage to be imperfect in our "bigger is better" society — they develop the capacity to grow and mature. Winning is not the only name of the game. Participating, cooperating, doing for others, feeling exhilaration — these become the important signposts on the journey of life. They are also the ingredients for increasing students' self-esteem.

Because encouraged students do not give up easily, they can and do ask others for help. They ask for personal information and demonstration, or they go to the tapes, disks, and books of information to "read up on it." In the philosophy of encouragement, mistakes are not seen as failures but as wrong numbers that come about from misdialing. In the film-making business, mistakes are exactly that: a "miss" of a "take." It simply means it has to be done again. When mistakes are viewed positively, they spur the learner on to become more critical in analysis and look at the situation through wider eyes. On the other hand, perfectionism robs the learner of "another try" because the learner realizes that he or she may never get "it." If they do get "it," "it probably won't be good enough for the teacher anyway." Perfectionism puts the learner in a no-win situation which is ultimately a losing situation. When mistakes are viewed as something horrendous, they infect and lead very quickly to discouragement. Moreover, the positive aspect of mistakes is that they consistently promote learning. Not a bad payoff for a task that did not turn out as we wanted it to. An ancient Chinese proverb says, "A child's life is like a piece of paper on which every passerby leaves a mark." Schools that care will leave marks of encouragement on our children.

Finally, encouragement teaches students to be asset finders rather than fault finders. As schools become environments of encouragement, positive things will happen. Imagine the excitement that will take place as students and teachers seek out and identify each others' talents. See the pride and wonder on all the faces in the student body as they list the talents of each member of the school and then share them with the whole community at a talent celebration. Someone will be a clown, someone a juggler, someone an artist, a musician, a dancer, a mime, a storyteller, a computer whiz, a poetess, a comedienne. As encouragement helps students and teachers alike become asset finders, schools in every community will be on natural highs, with positive attitudes the norm. Classrooms will be stimulating and creative places to which children will want to come. Encouragement may not teach a student to spell or make mathematical correlations, but without it, students and teachers will not be able to teach and learn. Both groups will be reduced to choosing sides in their power plays — quite a waste of teaching and learning power.

Wonder, Play, Creativity, and Celebration

Children who are admired and encouraged will be stimulated to wonder, to play, to be creative, and finally, to celebrate each and every moment of their lives. When these ways of nourishment are available to children, they consistently feel good about themselves, have high self-esteem, and have the ability to solve or rise above their problems. They view life more positively, and hence, they think and act in more positive ways.

Wonder

Ancient philosophers have always insisted that there is a basic attitude necessary for all wisdom. It is the attitude of wonder. Sam Keen says that wonder is a "prerequisite" for wisdom.[23] So strongly does he believe in wonder and its connection to wisdom that he recommends a course be taught in all schools entitled, "Silence, Wonder, And The Art of Surrender."[24] He says that a course in wonder would aid students in developing an inner silence, in letting go and letting be.[25] It would help them be at ease in situations in which surrender, rather than control, is appropriate. He even suggests that students who have participated in "a sojourn in silent exile . . . may have gained sufficient reverence for language to become outraged at chatter, propaganda, and noise."[26] Frequently parents and educators are dismayed because children, especially teenage children, listen to rock music with the volume turned very high. Rather than decry society for giving us rock music and teenage idols, parents and educators need to spend the necessary time nurturing children and students through wonder, through "a sojourn in silent exile," so that children's tastes can be developed.

Wonder is the ability to be astonished, to have awe aroused by something strange, miraculous, mysterious; to enter the darkness within to find the light. Matthew Fox speaks about the wonder of our bodies working completely in the dark and asks how we cannot but be filled with wonder at this "dark mystery worth meditating on."[27] He reminds us that:

> The sun does not penetrate all of space. Much of space is dark. Much of the birth of the cosmos itself was done in the dark—the sun has not always existed. The seed under ground is growing in the dark no less than the fetus in the mother's womb. All mystery is about the dark. All darkness is about mystery.[28]

Schools need to lead students to wonder. Through ritual done well students could learn the art of silence, the art of letting go of busyness, and of projecting themselves onto other persons or things, and the art of seeing light in the darkness. They need to experience the integration of body, mind, and world, especially since minds, rather than bodies, are taught in the classroom. They need to learn to read the language of the body, learn to acquire techniques of relaxation, and to enjoy their body. Little of this is learned in present physical education classes, which stress competitive winning over kinesthetic awareness and work to separate mind from body through dualism. Sam Keen says, "Education which avoids the erogenous zones, the sensitive areas, neglects the power structure . . . . it more properly deserves the name 'indoctrination.' [29]

Wonder gets us in touch with our power structure. This is important for children, especially adolescent children. They are full of energy, full of questions, full of willingness to seek out treasure from their living journey. Entering the dark and mysterious is not fearful for them, rather it is an adventure filled with fun and learning. Students can enter and practice wonder by the letting go of deep breathing, by getting in touch with the body's rhythms, "the music of one's body—its breath, the tympanum of one's heartbeat or lung beat," says Matthew Fox.[30] It is the letting go of all images, a movement from the here and now to the beyond which is within. It is precisely because we do not know what is there that the attitude of wonder leads to wisdom. Trusting the empty spaces, trusting the silences, the void, the unknown, will open educators and students to see and think differently, to learn the great truths which exist in the plants, the animals, humans, the unknown, the voids of the universe. Trusting the darkness, the mystery, will lead children and adults to ponder and play.

Play

Play has been called the very stuff of childhood, but more than this, it is the very stuff of living fully and creatively. Brian Swimme says, "The difference between humans and other primates (is) the ability of the human to make play its dominant activity throughout a lifetime."[31] Play enriches us and play must be part of the stuff of the classroom. Schools which incorporate play in the curriculum enable students to expand their minds, develop friendships more quickly, and develop a better ability to handle other relationships. This is because there is a dynamic in play which produces an ebb and flow whereby students learn "give and take" in a fun and acceptable way. Furthermore, play enlivens the content of learning and helps students in integration and connection-making. It challenges them and helps them to release their imagination and creativity.

Play is restricted in our culture in part because of the culture's love affair with dualism and the lifestyle that love-affair urges. The historical Puritan ethic of keeping busy "accomplishing" because "idle hands are the devil's workshop" does not allow for play. Ivan Illich reports a friend's comment on the problem: "The major obstacle on the way to a society that truly educates was well defined by a black friend of mine in Chicago, who told me that our imagination was 'all schooled up.'"[32] Play can help us change this, can help us get out of being "all schooled up."

Schools are perfect places for play. John Holt reminds us that "No one has to *do* anything in order to 'socialize' the children, or *make* them take part in the life of the group. They are born social, it is their nature."³³ Children are willing participants in play. We need only to give a minimal structure to their environment and get out of their way. Mary Caroline Richards says, "We have to realize that a creative being lives within ourselves, whether we like it or not, and that we must get out of its way, for it will give us no peace until we do."³⁴ When play finds more of a home in our schools, it will find more of a home in our environment.

Play can help transform the way we spend a great deal of our time, too. Because of our dualistic approach to life, American society is faced with some ongoing problems. The lack of play, coupled with the early introduction of television among our children, is one of them. We raise our children on television, use it as a pacifier for our babies, a sitter for our youngsters, and a source of negative energy for our adolescents. We have to ask seriously about the damage done to our children through television. Is life really a series of car chases, wrecks, killings, washing powders, toys, beer, and new car commercials? Are we aware that students who are frequent television watchers have little or no interaction with other human beings? By the time they reach the age of fifteen, they have averaged over 20,000 hours in front of the television; a passive, unchallenging and uncaring mode of spending time. Rarely is there any educational value in watching the major networks. However, the toll on children's muscular and skeletal systems, their brain development and diet, and their ability to think critically and interact, is enormous. In our culture TV is a thief: it steals meaningful conversation from our children, and it steals meaningful action and irretrievable hours from living. It replaces meaning with dullness and boredom. Commercials help to frustrate children, keeping them stirred up and appealing to their baser interests of consumerism with the message that more is better. TV helps stunt students' emotional, intellectual, and physical capacities, while it keeps them from appreciating ecology and their natural environment.

Play in school helps to reverse the effects of TV because play is not an end in itself. It is not a spectator sport nor the result of an activity or experience; rather it *is* the activity and the experience. It involves full participation, is spontaneous, requires improvisation, and leads to decision-making. Sue Spayth Riley says:

> Because there is no imposed blueprint, there is no right, no wrong, no fear of failure that results from trying to follow a pattern. There is freedom for decision-making.[35]

A. S. Neill says that play should be completely separated from learning: "I have a great objection to a teacher who comes along and sees a child playing with mud, and uses this as a chance to talk about coast erosion, or some nonsense like that . . . . Play to me means no strings attached at all."[36] It is tempting to want to agree with Neill's statement that play should be completely separated from learning, but on some levels play is a part of learning and learning is a part of play. Schools need to realize this. It is "both/and": *both* times of complete immersion in a fantasy world *and* times of unhurried exploration and experimentation with ideas, objects, toys, and materials. Schools can become the stage setting for play, providing equipment, materials, and necessary guidelines. The school environment of play has to be somewhat structured but never does the process of play itself need to be.[37] John Holt refers to the attitude of play in the classroom when he says that educators need to ". . . bring as much of the world as we can into the classroom; give children as much help and guidance as they need and ask for; listen respectfully when they feel like talking; and then get out of the way."[38] The generation of creative ideas through improvisation makes play flow; it happens when the doing comes from the inside. It cannot be programmed.

Play has important implications for both administrators and teachers. When these people are not playful they tend to become rigid and inflexible and to suffer from higher distress-related illnesses. Many educators see themselves as authorities and act in uptight ways. They have great difficulty in letting go so that play can happen. Sue Spayth Riley points out:

> Though well-meaning, the adult who interferes and suggests, "Why don't you do it this way?" or "Put that piece up here," or "Can't you figure that out?" is committing a kind of castration of childhood.[39]

Those who tend toward this kind of rigidity will find many reasons why play ought not to be a part of daily educational life.

However, they can be shown the folly of their ways by careful and caring colleagues so they can be brought aboard this important train of learning.

Although it will not be easy to bring play into the classroom, it need not take a revolution either. Any content to be taught can be better taught and more easily understood if placed in the context of play and experimentation. Teachers can ask the students how they think a particular lesson can be taught. Students are quite adept at imagining, initiating, and urging forward movement. Teachers who realize that play is in the doing will want their students to do the doing. The key is to let the lessons be play. This means removing the idea that it must be done a certain way, or it must be done "right."

Creativity

As students become doers in their own ways, their creative power gets released. The process of play deepens into the process of creativity, in which something new is brought into being. Something "pops up," as Rollo May describes it.[40] There is an exhilaration that accompanies a burst of creativity and a new feeling of power that sinks deeply into our personality. So rich are children in this faculty, that they come to school with creativity bursting out of their minds and hearts, shouting out through their speech and all their activities. From the colors they mix to the lines they draw, from the animals they name to the world in which they live, from the sounds they capture to the figuring out of who will be their friends, children reach deeply into themselves and rely on their creativity every day. When schools provide the environment of healthy soil, water, and sunlight for these gardens of creativity, they facilitate strong personal growth. The learning that develops from students' using their natural creativity will be astounding. The cures for cancer are in students' creativity. A more just world exists now in students' creativity. An understanding of and elimination of the root causes of poverty exist now in students' creativity. The ways around distress, the discovery of non-polluting technology, the ability for everyone to have a fair and equitable income, exist now in students' creativity. What is necessary is that this creativity be allowed to flourish during the years of compulsory education.

TRANSFORMING EDUCATION

Children begin their formal schooling straight out of some of the most creative and enhancing environments known. Throughout the country there are nursery schools, pre-schools, and kindergartens, many of the highest quality, where daily, young children express their creativity in momentous ways. This is true in both urban and rural settings. Many of these schools have very low overhead and they are usually funded privately by the parents whose children use them. In these centers of creativity teachers interact fully with the children as they work, play, and create, entering deeply into their world of reality and fantasy, seeing and understanding through their eyes. Frequently different from their counterparts in elementary and secondary education, nursery and pre-school teachers are unusually refreshing and characteristically "up." Viewing themselves more as orchestra leaders and less as disciplinarians, they work carefully to bring out what these creative children already have inside. They help the children make connections in their world and feel comfortable with it. These teachers feel encouraged in their work, and are delighted that they have these children in their charge. When a child draws a picture they are more prone to ask, "Would you like to tell me about your picture, Johnny?" than to ask, "What is it?" They realize that the latter question could be perceived as a criticism.

In contrast, many teachers beyond the first or second grades in elementary and in almost all of secondary education have accepted the "school is work" syndrome which all too seriously demands a curriculum and syllabus without play and minimizes the use of creativity and thoughtful interaction. Public schools have been concentrating on order in the classroom, an imposed discipline, a standardized but all too often haphazard curriculum, unrealistic achievement tests, and higher SAT scores as an end-product and proof of quality education. In turn this has helped to create most of the problems facing these institutions today. Neil Postman and Charles Weingartner rightfully ask: "Is that what we really want kids to learn?"[41] Schools need to allow and promote joy, excitement, and celebration of any and all learning in a leisurely atmosphere, based on a meaningful and global curriculum. No longer can play, creativity, exciting learning, and the interaction which stimulates new questions and new ideas, be left out. Sam Keen says: "If education neglects the intimate, the proximate, the sensuous, the autobiographical, the personal, it fails in its creative task and becomes only conservative, or perhaps reactionary."[42] Educators need to believe that every perception, every desire, every action undertaken in a playful and creative way, pays off in learning.

Celebration

The opposite of control is celebration. "Celebration is a forgetting in order to remember," says Matthew Fox. It is "a forgetting of ego, of problems, of difficulties."[43] Celebration is what happens when administrators and teachers let go of control. Hard words for both groups. There is such a strong tendency towards control and controlling behavior in American education that for many administrators and teachers letting go is indeed difficult—difficult but not impossible, and also very necessary. Without control being exercised by an authority figure the atmosphere can at once change to celebration. By letting go of control, it is not meant that things will be "out of control." What is being suggested here is not some kind of permissive mood of "do your own thing," but a celebrative environment where joy is possible, where difficulties are talked out, where cooperation is the norm, where mutual respect is fostered. An environment in which teachers and students together learn. An environment where song fills the air, excitement runs high, and affirmation is freely given. An environment where encouragement and trust reign. An environment which fosters touch, admiration, and celebration. An environment which would replace the straight rows, replace the dictatorial process of having to put one's hand up to be recognized (would any of us find this practice acceptable at our job?), replace the rigidly scheduled recess with a recess called forth by the kidneys or a needed change of pace.

Think back to some times when you genuinely had fun in your life. What were the components of that fun time?

Openness to the moment?

Letting go of all cares?

Letting be of any difficulties that surrounded you?

Laughing with your comrades?

Seeing situations as joyful, funny, amusing, jolly?

TRANSFORMING EDUCATION

> Building make-believe worlds where all was right and love reigned supreme?
>
> Holding hands with someone who was special?
>
> Being told you could help make the cookies or cook the pudding?
>
> Being accepted by the gang?
>
> Making paper dolls and brightly coloring them?
>
> Drinking milk and eating cookies?
>
> Being the voice of your favorite puppets?
>
> Making funny faces and laughing about them?
>
> Drinking carbonated soda pop and belching loudly?
>
> Recording the belches and playing them back for all your friends to hear?
>
> Singing at the top of your lungs?
>
> Shouting and being quiet?
>
> Playing with your favorite pet or pets?
>
> Reading books?
>
> Thinking about questions and answers?
>
> Telling jokes?

Can all of this be going on in the classroom and class work still be done? That is really the wrong question. The more accurate question is: can any class work be done when it is not done in a spirit of joy and celebration? As you just now read the list of fun times in your life and added your own examples, what happened to your spirit? Are you just a bit lighter now than you were before you read the list? Are you just a bit more open now than you were? What happened to your face when you chuckled at something humorous on the list? Is your mind just a bit more receptive now that your joyful mood allowed the neurons to move?

There have to be times of celebration, times of folk dancing, times of meaningful touch, times of shared joy for all of us to be able to learn, make connections, to absorb ideas and develop knowledge. There has to be a celebrative stance around education for it to make a difference. Without it, the creative juices which long to be called forth in each and every one of us, will stagnate and dry up. For too long our educational systems have been turning healthy, creative, wondering, fresh and alive, spontaneous human beings into prunes—all dried up! Celebrative classrooms with celebrating students and teachers will inspire, create, promote, and enable better learning. Fun is always a plus. Celebration is always a joy. Furthermore, it is a stress reducer. When our most technologically advanced hospitals and doctors offered Norman Cousins a few months to live he decided to laugh himself well for a lot longer time.[44] This is what education is about: each person taking care of him- or herself; taking control over his or her life and learning in every interaction. Lewis Thomas reminds us that:

> It is a distortion, with something profoundly disloyal about it, to picture the human being as a teetering, fallible contraption, always needing watching and patching, always on the verge of flapping to pieces.[45]

In *Encounter with the Self,* Donald E. Hamachek says, "Healthy people see themselves as liked, wanted, acceptable, able, and worthy. Not only do they feel that they are people of dignity and worth, but they behave as though they were."[46] It is up to the adult community to support our children, and through celebration to help them bring themselves into maturity and the journey towards wisdom.

Choices and Consequences

In 1979 the International Year of the Child was celebrated. Sponsored by the World Health Organization, one of the issues it looked at was what is the meaning of functional adulthood. The World Health people came up with some non-culturally-biased measures to apply to the data. One of their questions was at what age does the typical young person in the American culture become capable of meeting the day-to-day requirements of an adult? Stephen Glenn, who summarized some of their findings says:

> . . . the average age of maturity for all urbanized, technologically advanced nations of the world other than the United States

was 16 to 17 years of age. For the United States it was 24 years of age.[47]

This means that it takes as much as "eight years longer to achieve the same level of functional adulthood or maturity in the United States than in any other comparable nation on earth."[48] He states further that moral and ethical development takes four years longer in the United States than in any other culture:

> Early on our students have the most sophisticated perceptions on earth about drinking, self-medication, casual sex and violence while at the same time they have the least developed internal controls.[49]

They wind up with no way to sort out the bombardment of perceptions, which shows up statistically in horrifying figures. In 1982 alone, 30,600 young people destroyed themselves through homicide, suicide, and accidental death due to drinking and driving. He continues, "the statistics show quite clearly that the United States has become one of the most dangerous places on earth to pass through the teenage years."[50]

These are very telling statements. There is a tremendous gap in our culture. On the one hand there is the enormous advocacy of sophisticated behavior while on the other hand there is the absence of adult and cultural controls and limits. This coupled with grossly inadequate judgmental maturity produces a chaos in the ways we parent and educate our children. To bridge the gap we need a moral and ethical breakthrough, a cultural leap. According to Glenn, whether a child can make the moral or ethical leap frequently depends on how much non-threatening dialogue the child has had with dad, mom, and teachers. After age seven or eight, the rate of maturation in most students is almost exclusively a dialectical function of experience and dialogue with more mature people, especially with adults. When peers have dialogue only with peers and not with adults, there is no upward movement in their judgmental maturity. Without adult dialogue there is a tendency to have the same level of insight over and over again, resulting in suppression of the maturing process. It is clear that when children at home and students in the classroom have meaningful and encouraging interactions with adults, rather than being commanded to see things the way a parent or teacher wishes them to see things, they will be better able to develop judgmental maturity. Armed with this skill, students will feel empowered and have the means necessary to match the satiating bombardment of information and choices pulsating in the culture.

This kind of empowerment derives from making choices based on experience which provides us with the deepest learning. Denying young people the experiences they can handle keeps them from both learning and becoming empowered. Sue Spayth Riley says:

> Adults, having learned so much from long experience, often find it difficult to give children defined areas of choice and then stand back and allow them to use their freedom.[51]

And A. S. Neill says: "Children should find things out for themselves. They shouldn't be told that Beethoven is better than Ellington."[52]

Participate in any driver education class in any high school in the nation, and you will see learning by experience in full bloom. You will also see motivation at its height and an openness and willingness to learn more. Students will go through hours of theory because even in the classroom, they feel the thrill of being "behind the wheel," whether at the driving simulator or just in their mind's eye. They have the opportunity to become closer to other students because of the small clusters that they form for assignment of the cars. Moreover, they function better working in groups because they get and give immediate feedback on their progress. "That was a dumb turn, Roger!" "Hey, way to go, Marie." They also know that if they do not study the theory, they will not be allowed to practice driving the car. The consequences of actions in driver education classes are always clear, spelled out in advance and given in an up-front manner. Furthermore, these consequences are always accepted, even by students who have been labeled "difficult." That is how powerful driver education is.

There is a great lesson to be learned here. It is simply this: let students get inside something, give them an opportunity to touch, to feel, to talk about, to get excited about — in short, to experience, and they willingly learn every time. Viola Spolin, in her book on improvisation, says:

TRANSFORMING EDUCATION

> We learn through experience and experiencing, and no one teaches us anything. If the environment permits it, anyone can learn what he chooses to learn; and if the individual permits it, the environment will teach him everything it has to teach.[53]

Spolin declares that "anyone can learn what he chooses to learn" and that is true in the present example. When is the last time any one of us heard about a student failing driver education? It seldom happens. Why? When students can see themselves doing something, when they can get a hands-on experience, make decisions for themselves, get in there and get dirty with it so to speak, they get interested, remain interested, and they learn. When they take an active part and experience something, they are more willing to do the leg work that goes with what is being taught. Finally, when they see a payoff that they can believe in, they will stay with it every time.

This is true for other classes, too. If we want our students to be interested and lively we must allow them to experience their surroundings through imagination, wonder, and discovery. Furthermore, we must allow them to share these experiences in a classroom or any other setting. Peter M. Kalellis says:

> Parents, teachers, clergy, peers, and people in power have unwittingly conspired to produce a large number of timid souls. However naive and innocent parents may be in censoring children who decide to express themselves, they are hindering a most important emotional apparatus—decision-making.[54]

We all learn from each other, from hearing other ideas, and from hearing similar ideas expressed differently by others. Having the chance to think and then share the fruit of that thinking, to feel and then tell others what our feelings are, to sense and make connections—all in a caring and safe environment—this is the process of experiencing. Memorizing facts which fill the pages of a history book misses the feeling of history. Being told rather than being asked stimulating questions minimizes any hope for discovery. Sitting five or more hours per day in a classroom in itself can be an act of cruelty. It becomes even more so when students are lectured to for most of that time, unable to move around at will, unable to claim another part of the classroom space. When students are denied the chance to be in small groups, to hear other opinions, when they are not asked to express their opinions, they get the message that their experiences are not worth validating and that they themselves are not worthwhile. Students who are given the freedom to explore their world through interactions with others, through the joys and sorrows of precious moments in their lives, through all forms of art and academic learning, and through their family and friends, discover much about themselves and their relationship to their environment. Moreover, experiencing, choosing, judging, deciding, and confronting, enables them to develop their self-esteem and to raise their level of maturity. This is why life-skills education and group process is so important for administrators and teachers. When these people are not at home with the dynamics of group interactions, when they have not checked their listening and encouragement skills in many years, when they have faulty teacher beliefs, they wreak havoc on students. Frequently they become an academic judge and jury, viewing their schools and classrooms as a court. When students are denied the freedom to express themselves in a meaningful way, when they are not listened to, not asked their opinion, they often look to antisocial ways for expressing their ideas and feelings. When students are valued and participate in a learning environment which offers a maximum amount of freedom, where they know what is expected of them, know the consequences, can make decisions, and live with the consequences without adult interference, their learning gets maximized. Don Dinkmeyer, Sr., Don Dinkmeyer, Jr., and Gary McKay ask teachers:

> Would you be happy within a system of policies and guidelines you had no part in developing? Your students also dislike dictatorships . . . . Learning to make decisions is an important part of education, a vital preparation for adulthood.[55]

Making decisions implies making choices. This natural ability to choose includes every aspect of school. Choosing enables students to take full responsibility for themselves, to live more enriched lives, and to deal better with authority. Accustomed to thinking, to seeing alternatives, to accepting consequences, they grow more honest with themselves and exercise more honesty in their interactions. This is self-responsibility at its highest level. Imagine a teenager saying to a police officer, "Yes, I was speeding. I was going twelve miles per hour over the speed limit. Yes, I'll take the ticket." Allowed to choose, students become better equipped to handle all situations which come into their lives.

Learning through choice needs to be one of the ways the new school system functions. In a choosing environment not surrounded by rules, regulations, commands, demands, and prohibitions, teachers and students can carve out a code of conduct satisfying for all. A. S. Neill, who pioneered the English Summerhill School based on a philosophy of love of children, says, "Our school is run on self-government, and the children are the ones that govern. We have law-breakers here as in any system, but they keep the laws better."[56] Sitting down eye-to-eye with each other, teachers and students can mutually come to workable compromises and decisions with which all can be happy. Choosing allows educators to trust students. Lecturing, moralizing, commanding, and demanding does not work nor does it promote a sense of responsibility. Helping to prepare students for their future means encouraging them now to exercise the natural energy of choosing. In an age of much information, choosing is of great importance. However, to make meaningful choices students need to have well developed skills of judgment. They need to know how to estimate and judge the effects of choices which are all around them. Without judging skills, meaningful choices become difficult and the sea of information will breed confusion rather than insight. Students need to be able to estimate the distance, rate of speed, and amount of time it takes to stop either an ocean-going tanker or a car. They need to learn judgment in using their time, choosing their friends, earning and spending their money, determining their hours of sleep, their food and drink, their reading materials and grade level, and controlling their habits. When students wisely use judgment they have at their command skills which could both one day help save their life, as well as daily help them choose the meaningful and necessary over the trivial and dispensable. Clark Moustakas supports this point:

> The challenge of authentic choice is a real challenge today because the values of the school and society are, in many respects, geared to successful achievement and a high place in the social hierarchy.[57]

When judging skills and choice are not a part of the schools' curriculum or of family life, when there is pressure to compete, society suffers and students will be doomed to continue to make their choices alone without meaningful adult input. When choice and judging skills are part of school and family life, opportunities for positive student-teacher and parental interaction are present, and self-esteem for everyone is increased. The ability to be honest with oneself and one's community, to make decisions and honor them, also increases.

Students who are definite and clear about their ability to make decisions live with less distress. When students are not allowed to make their own decisions, they lose the ability to function; their life is lived in a semi-dark tunnel. Jean Liedloff remarks that "Americans are perhaps the most carefully protected children in history." Because of this she says that they are "the least *expected* to know how to look after themselves." She speaks further of the importance of self responsibility, with parents and teachers being willing to step back so that children can look after themselves:

> The operative factor seems to be placement of responsibility. The machinery for looking after themselves, in most Western children, is in only partial use, a great deal of the burden having been assumed by adult caretakers.[58]

Every decision made for a student is a robbery made against the student's store of self. Students who are kept from decision-making ultimately believe they are inadequate. They select mistaken goals for their behavior and become dependent.[59] Conversely, students who are decision-makers become empowered. Other skills come more easily to decision-makers because they realize that any learning is on their own shoulders. They know what they know, and they know what they do not know. They know that if they want to know something, they are going to have to find out how they can learn it. John Holt says:

> What is essential is to realize that children learn independently, not in bunches; that they learn out of interest and curiosity, not to please or appease the adults in power; and that they ought to be in control of their own learning, deciding for themselves what they want to learn and how they want to learn it.[60]

Students who are decision-makers see with a sharper focus because in their comprehension they see interconnections. They build upon what they already know and understand.

Decision-making skills also open students to the world of ethics. They become more capable of making choices based on ethical values, more capable in helping to establish a genuine morality. Sue Spayth Riley speaks of the decision-making process and its relationship to students and their place in a democratic society:

> . . . too often the public school system fails to build on children's earlier experiences and instead, for the sake of order and efficiency perhaps, limits rather than extends decision-making. If we are raising children to become free men and women capable of participating intelligently in a democratic society, one may well question this lockstep approach to learning.[61]

If students are to become adults who live out of moral principles and who make ethical decisions, it will be necessary for educators to realize that decision-making in the areas of values and life skills is an integral part of the educational process. Educators are going to have to declare their own values, manifest their own decision-making skills and offer their own experiences of choosing.

What is being proposed here is not utter freedom, which cannot exist, but the "both/and" of the dialectic: freedom and responsibility. All choices involve a "letting go" of something, a freedom "from" to have a freedom "for." Affirming freedom in this light implies an equally affirming responsibility which together empowers students and offers them a fuller participation in life.

5

Enabling Educational Health

Honoring Temperaments and Difference

Accepting difference in people is frequently difficult. Often we falsely conclude that difference in temperament and behavior is the result of some malady, perhaps even badness or stupidity. We prefer to believe that people are fundamentally alike even though they are not. We do not like to accept the fact that people have preferred ways of being and model their behavior on these preferences.

Jung points out that people exercise preference in functioning. He calls this preference "function types" or "psychological types." He posits four differences: introversion versus extraversion, sensation versus intuition, thinking versus feeling, and judgment versus perception. Isabel Myers and Katheryn Briggs have built on Jung's work and devised the Myers-Briggs Type Indicator, a widely used tool for identifying sixteen different patterns which show how people act. In understanding differences, Jung does not say that a person is either one or the other of these four pairs. Rather, one can be to some degree extraverted or introverted, thinking or feeling, and so on. Jung also holds that one can change towards another preference, and that the preferences become stronger upon using them and weaker with disuse.

Adler, a contemporary of Jung, believes that because human beings are social they select behaviors based on how they wish to belong, to be accepted. He speaks of goals for behavior, chief among them being power, chosen either for negative or positive gain. Rudolf Dreikurs has built upon his work and today Adlerian psychology—a school which urges encouragement, self responsibility and common sense—enjoys high esteem worldwide, especially among educators and parents.

Almost twenty-five hundred years ago Hippocrates spoke of four temperaments—choleric, phlegmatic, melancholic, and sanguine. Temperament was seen as the place where individual spirit and heredity blend. Building on this notion, René M. Querido speaks of children's temperaments:

> Children's moods are associated with the seasons. Some children are summer children—not because they were born in the summer, but because their gestures and characteristics show an affinity with summer. Some children are fiery like the summer, others watery like the winter; some are earthbound like the fall, while some are light and airy like the spring.[1]

These patterns or preferences offer clues about personalities, and this knowledge can be a great help to educators. Knowing that someone who is calm can also be fearful, someone determined can also be domineering, an outgoing student can also be undisciplined, a student exhibiting idealism can also exhibit criticism and unsociability, can help teachers and administrators understand students. Although there is a danger in believing they have someone figured out, saying for example, "she's introverted" or "he's phlegmatic," it is far less dangerous than forgetting or denying that these patterns exist and expecting all students to function in only one way.

Difference and preference also show up in the ways students learn, becoming more pronounced in adolescents and adults. Anthony F. Gregorc and Helen B. Ward have found that adolescents and adults acquire and order information in specific ways.[2] In acquiring information some prefer a more abstract and some a more concrete way. In ordering information some prefer a sequential pattern, while others prefer a more random pattern. Gregorc and Ward have found that the thinking and ordering patterns form four distinct learning preferences. They call these abstract sequential, abstract random, concrete sequential, and concrete random. Every person studied reveals use of all four ways, but at least 90% express a definite preference for one or two methods of acquiring information. They conclude that certain teaching styles more closely approximate certain learning preferences.

Gregory Bateson illustrates the relationship between teaching styles and learning preference by telling about two different teaching tasks which occurred simultaneously in the 1950s. He was teaching psychiatric residents at a hospital and artists at a school of fine arts. He asked the residents for definitions of the terms "sacrament" and "entropy," and asked the artists to convince him that a cooked crab he gave them was indeed the remains of a living thing. "I was offering my class the core notions of 2,500 years of thought about religion and science . . . . Of course, the question set for the psychiatrists was the *same question* as that which I set for the artists: Is there a biological species of entropy?"[3] Bateson knew that different audiences required different teaching approaches. However, it is not only audiences that differ; it is the very people who make up the audience. Hence, teachers need to develop different styles of teaching, they need to vary their styles, and they need to develop a willingness to co-teach with those who have other styles.

Whatever teaching style is used, it is important to realize that experimentation is a wise teacher and the outcome will always be instructive to both teachers and students. In this sense, whatever happens will be fruitful. If educators are fearful of experiment they will be keeping themselves from freshness and vitality in their teaching. As they experiment with teaching styles they will begin to see patterns and be better able to structure their teaching plans.

Why have schools not dealt better with admitting, understanding, and serving the differences which have always existed? First, dualism and viewing education as an industry precludes honoring difference. When teachers have to deal with a new group of students each year, have to teach between twenty-five and one-hundred-fifty students a day, and have to satisfy a demanding system, they do not spend much time reflecting on difference and temperament in their charges. Rather, they prepare a lesson and hope that their students "get it." For those who do not—and their numbers are substantial—the official school jargon is that "they" do not want to learn. In this system of education it becomes almost impossible for teachers and administrators to know how each student experiences class work and material, or how a student experiences him or herself.

Secondly, the tendency to streamline in education and in parenting prevents honoring individual differences. We think all people like orange juice for breakfast and cookies and milk for a snack. Routine lectures and assignments become easier to present. However, as students, parents, educators, and people from the community capture a new vision and together work with it, curriculum and pedagogy can be built in more meaningful ways. Schools can become the centers of facilitation where staff are enablers in the lives of their students. In this way all do the learning and all reap the benefits. Paulo Freire says that the program content of education comes from a combination of reality and the people themselves:

> . . . the generative theme cannot be found in men divorced from reality, nor yet in reality divorced from men, much less in "no man's land." It can only be apprehended in the men-world relationship.[1]

Some might argue that Freire's ideas only pertain to adults and are not relevant to early or secondary education; but this is not true. Ideas either are relevant across the board, or they are irrelevant across the board. It is the adaptation of ideas to a meaningful curriculum and to different temperaments that helps empower students. Freire says that "man's thinking about reality and man's action upon reality and how he works out of that reality — praxis — is what is important."[5] Put another way, the curriculum must spark a fire which ignites the tinder deep inside the inner recesses of students' minds, hearts, and emotions. Educators need to find meaningful methodology for the presentation of content. The great resources to be tapped in all of this are the students and teachers themselves. The aspirations, motives, and objectives which Freire speaks of are occurring consistently within them. David Kiersey and Marilyn Bates suggest that teachers should frequently ask themselves about their students. "What *kind* of person am I encountering, and on that basis what sort of messages from me will define the relationship in a facilitative and productive way?"[6] This kind of questioning makes possible the "drawing out" that is education. It also takes into account mood and change. Sid Simon suggests that principals should ask their teachers: "What do you need from me?" This is an excellent question for teachers to make their own and ask of their students. The information gleaned from these kinds of questions will give teachers what they need to know about a student's temperament and goals at the moment.

Teachers are facilitators of the learning process. They help students confront deep questions, give and find information, and help them organize and express their thought in art and word. They urge them on to make a praxis out of their thought and to work towards their own transformation. They are less responsible *for* their students, more *to* them. Rather than take charge of them, they respond to them, move towards them. Kiersey and Bates observe, "There isn't any way you can really understand me, but if you stop trying to change me to look like you, you might come to *appreciate* me."[7] This must be part of the creed of education, to appreciate and love our children, no matter their temperaments, no matter their rhythms.

Developing Creative Learning Environments

A deep and caring relationship between teachers and students is necessary for learning to take place. Students consistently need to feel important, capable, in control of their own learning, and be in an environment which supports this.

The more educators begin to see students as individuals with their own ways of being, behaving, and delighting, the more effective education will become. Educators need to believe that children are people now, worthy of being accorded mutual respect, honor, and esteem. Educators have to erase permanently from their vocabulary and thinking, terms and distinctions which are roadblocks that detour student initiative. Imagine a family in which one adult told another adult who had cooked a dinner, "It was good, but you could have done better"; "You could have tried harder"; "I want you to do better the next time." When educators say these things or label children as smart or not smart, or as a person with problems, they are putting them down, teaching them to feel inferior. Furthermore, these put-downs work in students to produce feelings of guilt, unhealthy competitiveness, and inadequacy. When students have problems, they need to know that the environment is safe for them to ask for help. Asking for help, which is looked upon negatively in our culture, is really a sign of strength and independence and should be encouraged. When educators view students' problems as clues, they learn more about their students. Problems can be beneficial, shedding light on what is presently needed by the student. They are opportunities to use creativity and to celebrate diversity. When adults want to eliminate problems or jump in to "solve" students' problems, they rob them of valuable opportunities in decision-making and living with consequences.

In a system of education called *Workshop Way,* Grace Pilon suggests that the classrooms of America be built from the ground up with the real needs of the student in mind. She is not lobbying for fancy rooms or the best in innovative school buildings. In fact, most of her forty years of teaching have been in the inner-city schools of this nation, which are proportionately more run-down than other school buildings. What she does deem essential in the school building is not bricks and mortar but the availability of freedom, creativity, and openness in the rooms and learning areas where we place students. "The room needs to be completely student oriented. Students need to know clearly the physical organization of the classroom. This clear cut vision of order . . . and mastery over the environment in the room make the place non-threatening,"[8] she counsels. Further, she suggests that many of the learning materials be of a hands-on nature, and that they be made by the teachers who will use them so they will sense their importance and be willing to use them daily. She believes the social conditioning of the classroom must be such that it can help create many positive relationships among and between students and teachers throughout the day, and that students themselves can handle personality clashes. Finally, there is an open door policy for parents to come into the classroom any time.

Workshop Way is being used in all grades from pre-school to university. The following stories give a flavor of how younger children learn from this innovative system. A kindergarten child is on the floor totally absorbed in working a thinker project, deciding where to put certain cards. A visitor approaches, sees the child's work and says, "My, but you're smart." Kim looks up at the adult without any sign of being overwhelmed by the compliment and says, "Everybody's smart in this room." Another story deals with

Jane and a first-grader who walked by her desk, saw her work, and informed her it was all wrong. "Jane's reply without anger or unhappiness was, 'WELL! My brain does not have to work like your brain!'"[9]

Both Kim and Jane had developed the skill of self-confidence. In order to learn well academically and to maintain emotional health while doing it, students need confidence in human skills and powers. They need to be convinced early in their educational growth that they can take charge of themselves and do what they need to do in their own behalf. Learning environments must foster this. They must also be conducive to thinking, listening, seeing, hearing, touching, and especially talking. Many educators erroneously believe that talking ought not to be a part of the learning atmosphere. Imagine being at a job all day and just listening, never speaking, never talking it over with colleagues. Much learning comes about by talking; to leave this out of the learning environment is to leave out a lot. The learning environment must also foster skills to make life more human. Among these are motivation, initiative, and independence in work and study habits. It takes courage to risk in order to learn, and honesty to face what one knows and does not know. Students have to know inside themselves that they can ask for help, that they can make decisions and accept consequences, and that they are able to control the starting and stopping of certain activities throughout the class day.

The "Workshop" part of *Workshop Way* system is an active, hands-on schedule of tasks which students perform every day whenever they are not in a didactic encounter with teachers. They choose from the posted tasks hung on the wall and assume the responsibility to do the tasks according to their understanding of them.[10] The first half hour of the day in grades one through eight is used to allow children complete freedom to begin the day independently of teachers. This not only gives the children anchors in the classroom but allows each student to move at his or her own pace. While the student is following the workshop, the teacher is freed to deal individually with other students, listening to them read, hearing homework, or in small learning clusters, grouped according to temperaments, teaching them a lesson.

Workshop Way enhances teacher-student relationships and fosters learning through trust. Students come to realize quite soon that everyone is different and there is no worry about where one is on the workshop schedule. Knowing what comes next throughout the day keeps students from feeling threatened. Students tend to be more relaxed because there are no controls or disciplinary fears placed over them. They know no one will laugh at them. It is also easier to create a "growing" climate at home as teachers share the philosophy of the classroom with parents. Students are free to reveal themselves in a real way, not covered up or masked over. Handling work in their own way in a supportive process with teachers and parents, with everyone apprised of what is happening, helps to create a rich atmosphere for students' learning. With outside and inside pressures eliminated, they are not only free to learn at their own pace, but they retain more, do not need reviews, and when the inevitable testing comes, score remarkably higher. In an interview, Grace Pilon tells of her first year teaching the *Workshop Way* in the St. Paul public schools:

> Our kids did so well in pre and post tests . . . that the director of research said, "We can't use those scores, we'll wait until September and give them another test . . . [to] see where they really are." Well I was tickled because I knew their scores would only go higher![11]

She attributes the high test scores to the *Workshop Way's* emphasis on human development. She believes that wherever children go, they are learning. She says further:

> We also never review. We find that when children learn in a relaxed atmosphere, they retain the content. We're actually doing something to the brain cells of these kids! We're changing the quality of mental energy.[12]

It is obvious from these quotes that atmosphere and methodology are important ingredients in learning. This does not mean that content is second class or that there can never be standards, guidelines, and expectations. However, it speaks strongly about the need for learning environments to be loving and caring. If, from time to time, a student feels out of sorts and shows problematic behavior, this simply means that the student needs more human development, to be taken aside for an extra amount of love and care. When this is given, especially in the form of listening and dialogue, the student can quickly return to the regular program of events. As students move along in human development and reach increased potential, discipline problems fade away and frequently are permanently dissolved. If discipline problems seem to persist, it is a major tip-off that there is something wrong with the *system,* not the student. It becomes the challenge of teachers, administrators, and parents to recognize and then satisfy new growth needs in students' learning.

While parents and educators like to recognize special talents and gifts, they need to be careful not to emphasize curriculum over human development. This frequently happens in talented and gifted programs. Some hard questions need to be asked. What message gets sent to these students about their inner selves? What does it mean to be placed in a talented and gifted program because some school systems hold up the accumulation of certain types of knowledge as special? How are the life and social skills necessary for full development implemented by these students? What message is sent to students who are not members of this club?

All students tend to need the same nourishment for personal, mental, social, and spiritual growth. We do a disservice to students when we place any label on them. Those who can excel in specific areas need increased challenges in those areas. The understanding of knowledge and the desire to wonder is a celebration for all, not just a few. If students are encouraged in school from their first day of enrollment, if they are in consistently positive learning environments and in a meaningful relationship with their teacher, they will get the basics in subject matter during their early years of elementary education. After that, all students need to be given the chance to study from the broadest possible curriculum, including the classics of history, understanding the world's cultures and foreign languages, as well as what personally interests them. They need to be fully engaged and encouraged to develop all their talents. Together, fully engaged teachers, administrators, and students make education an exciting and enriching process.

The Differently-Abled is Us

In the last two decades mainstreaming has placed many students who are handicapped in regular classrooms. This has resulted in more students becoming aware of people who are "different," and many parents and students are taking sides on the mainstreaming issue. While the handicapped themselves are frequently not asked to be part of the discussion, for some parents and students it takes on all the steam of a debate and for others a spirit of genuine dialogue. There still exists in technological America a distinct distaste for those who are different. Although attitudes are changing, prejudice against the handicapped continues to be high. The consensus of thought is that only specialists can teach handicapped people. One teacher training manual states, "Teaching handicapped students requires special training." It then goes on to list six points that teachers need to know:[13]

1. An overview of Public Law 94-142.

2. The various categories of handicaps, such as emotionally disturbed, hearing impaired, physically impaired, learning disabled, and so on.

3. The flow chart for referrals from their own district.

4. How to write an IEP (Individualized Education Program) according to their district guidelines.

5. Where to find curriculum materials to meet the handicapped student's needs.

6. How to handle severe behavior problems.

Public Law 94-142 is part of The Education For All Handicapped Children Act of 1975 and states in part:

> Each state must have "in effect a policy that assures all handicapped children the right to a free appropriate public education," and must develop a plan which details the policies and procedures which insure the provision of that right . . . and must insure that local educational agencies . . . will establish the individualized educational programs required by this Act.[14]

Outside of teachers' knowing this law, the other five points mentioned above are things that all teachers—not just teachers of the handicapped—would profit by knowing. Education should not foster the myth of specialization. In most schools today once certain students are seen as slow learners, or learning disabled, or handicapped, it becomes easy to script them and have fixed expectations — usually quite low — for them. Most adults relate differently toward them than toward "normal" students, usually expecting less from the handicapped, more from the "normals," and much more from the "gifted." The following quote from a teacher training manual illustrates the problem:

> Special education is now interpreted to mean the individualized education program (IEP). It employs a variety of techniques, procedures, instructional materials, and equipment to advance the student's rate of cognitive, affective, and motor development. Special education recognizes that all handicapped students have a wide range of educational needs, varying greatly in intensity and duration.[15]

Is this not what regular education is supposed to recognize? Certainly students profit from individualized education. A look at the phenomenal success of many alternative schools and learning centers shows the benefits of a more individualized approach. All teaching must employ a variety of techniques, procedures, and instructional materials if education is to speak to students. It is hoped that all education would be interested in student's cognitive, affective, and motor development. Finally, every part of education — certainly not just special education — must recognize that every student is differently-abled and has a wide range of educational needs, varying greatly in intensity and duration.

There are indeed some students who require a particular space, time, or food plan to accommodate their circumstances. However, serious questions have to be asked about the umbrella that special education claims to protect. All of us suffer from emotional disturbances from time to time. Some of us may have hearing, sight, or physical impairments. Some may be unable to learn as quickly as others, but all of us do learn what we need to, many in spite of systems which hold us back. Moreover, numerous students could take on the task of helping a sight-impaired student with learning, and in return learn some important things about themselves and a different way in which to view the world. We do great disservice to both the "handicapped" and the "normals" when we insist upon labels which separate. There are some students whose impairment requires the aid of a specialized staff. These people are better served in special schools. But the vast majority of "special" students in our public schools need and want to be treated as part of the gang. To their credit teacher trainers

Don Dinkmeyer, Sr., Don Dinkmeyer, Jr., and Gary McKay call for treating students differently but not differentially:

> We must not lose sight of the fact that these students, like all students, are *whole* persons. They function according to beliefs (private logic) and purposes (goals), as do all human beings. Those who attempt to explain special students' behavior with special theories which do not apply to the so-called "normal" population do these students a disservice.[16]

These authors make an important point. Many have felt the effects of special theories and labels which have been responsible for exclusion from certain groups, jobs, and ways of living. Such exclusion was practiced on a large scale with native American peoples, with slavery, and with the Holocaust in Nazi Germany. It is still being done against women and minorities. Differences need to be recognized but more importantly they need to be accepted. Because school is usually the first place where we become aware of major differences in our world, it is an excellent place to learn acceptance. We come face to face with those who see things differently, act differently, speak differently, and think differently. As we learn to welcome these differences in our lives, our personalities become enhanced.

There is a strong tendency in American society to disengage from what we perceive as difficult. This is reflected in our language and use of terms. The use of the term "handicap" is quite revealing. Originally, it referred to a game in which forfeits were drawn from a cap or hat. By way of extension, it has come to refer to the physically or mentally disabled. It is one way we have of naming what for many is a difficult subject. Some people may speak of themselves using the term "handicapped," but terms can become labels which keep people down. Labels rarely name situations accurately, and sometimes those who have been labeled spend the rest of their lives trying to put the label behind them. People may be better served if the term "handicapped" were changed to "differently-abled."[17] "Differently-abled" brings us closer to the truth of what it is to be human. Precisely what is missing from the term "handicapped" is that it offers nothing of what it is to be human. It is a name applied to a group rather than an explanation of who the people are, how they see themselves, and how they wish to be seen by others. "Differently-abled" supports a person's uniqueness while not masking or denying that the person is different. In a sense, "differently-abled" builds esteem in each of us.

Using the term differently-abled will help educators use language which describes and names in positive ways. It will also help them to perceive all students as learners. Some differently-abled students may be slow learners, disabled, underachievers, or hyperactive. Some may suffer impairment, having an absence of fingers, toes, or limb, loss of hearing or eyesight, a severed nerve, a weak heart, or other malfunctioning organ. Because of this they may be disabled in some degree. They may even have a handicap, impairment, or disability that interferes with normal living. But as the Dinkmeyers and Gary McKay remind us "Handicap is highly personal; it describes an individual's own reactions to the presence of an impairment or disability."[18] All have the capacity to learn.

Learning for mentally disabled students may happen in a less abstract and more concrete way, but many of these students can be part of a regular classroom. Through peer encouragement in the classroom, through being included in school activities and being accepted as whole human beings, the mentally disabled will be in good hands with their fellow students. Many times these fellow students can become speech, physical, and occupational therapists and counselors to the mentally disabled. This may be the best preparation there can be to help the mentally disabled take their place side by side with the rest of the population during childhood and in adulthood. These students learn more slowly, but they are neither incompetent nor incapable. Seeing them as differently-abled encourages normal patterns of interaction with them. In the process we become aware of their significance as they become aware of ours. Together the mentally disabled and the non-disabled can be both givers and receivers of learning, helping to create meaning in life.

In speaking about slow learners the Dinkmeyers and McKay say that materials should be presented simply, with directions clear and brief. They say further that "slow learners need encouragement to change their behavior; they may constantly lose their pencils, misplace their papers, and in general be disorganized."[19]

Frankly, all of us need to have things presented simply, with directions clear and brief. All of us need encouragement to change behaviors; witness those who want to give up smoking, lose weight, learn a new skill. Many of us misplace pencils and papers, and the great majority of extremely creative people are disorganized in some areas. The point is, if we want to insist upon labeling some students as slow learners, we should be prepared to look in the mirror and do a lot of laughing. Many college professors and many intellectual lights at the best-run companies cannot find paper and pencil or much else in their laboratories or on their desks. There is a story about how Einstein, when asked his phone number, went to the phone book and looked it up. Edison was labeled learning disabled. His mother took him out of school so he could create at home.

Some slow learners may be pseudo-slow learners. These students are not slow learners but claim it as a defense mechanism to get through their years of schooling. They have varied IQ scores but act as if they cannot learn, usually because it gets them special attention and special service from adults. They dominate the family and the classroom and are remarkable at using their "deficiencies." They have learned to use "the system" and show great potential in creativity and leadership.

Similar to the pseudo-slow learners but usually more angry and manipulative, are students who are underachievers. They frequently score in the top third of their class but feel unsuccessful and make poor grades. Linnus Pecaut places them in four different categories: the dependence seeker, the independence seeker, the approval seeker, and the security seeker.[20] What they have in common is the shifting of responsibility away from themselves and onto others, usually adults. These students use their passive apathetic behavior as a subtle form of power. Francis X. Walton says their private logic goes like this:

> You . . . are going to tell us what to do, when to do it, and how to do it. It's clear that we can't change anything. We can't fight city hall, so I'll tell you what you can do, Mr./Ms. Teacher. You can have it! It's your classroom. It's your school. On the other hand I want to get out of this place some day, so I'll do enough academic work to get by (that's for me). You can bet I won't do any more than enough to get by (that's for you).[21]

Buried beneath these attitudes and beliefs are feelings of being lost, uncared for, unloved. In many of their most negative interactions underachievers are calling out loudly for adults who will trust them, who will believe in them, who will tell them they are significant. Students who have been taught that their only commodity is their deficiency need to be encouraged and believed in especially by the adult community. Some adults may feel that difficulties students have are far more severe than positive attention and encouragement can treat. Rarely is this true. Where individualized instruction exists, where students have meaningful relationships with teachers and with their parents, emotional difficulties either do not occur or are quickly healed. The Dinkmeyers and McKay state:

> . . . emotional tensions, aggressiveness, anxious behavior, and other disturbing symptoms seem to disappear when encouraging remedial techniques are used and the student begins to achieve in school.[22]

When schools remove the pressure to excel which fosters unhealthy competition, and substitute a relaxed pace, students will be able to concentrate on learning. The truth is that underachievers are angry with their school, their parents, other adults, and society. Sometimes they perceive refusing to learn, using insults, and defeating others, as the only way they can use power.

Another group of students frequently mislabeled are the hyperactives. Usually "hyperactivity" says more about the person using the term than it does about someone's behavior. Many of us have short attention spans when we are doing something we do not like to do. We fidget around, daydream, and flit from place to place. We have fairly long attention spans when we like what we are doing. How many of us spend hours and even days agonizing and catastrophizing over the filling out and filing of income tax forms but enjoy every quiet minute of a best seller which may require many late nights to finish? Hyperactive students need challenges and need to be heard. They are full of ideas, full of plans which need the freedom to be expressed. Usually the last thing they need is a drug to slow them down. The rest of us need to learn to live with them and be thankful for their energy.

It may be helpful to know that few professionals in the psychological community agree on the terms, etiology, diagnosis, or treatment of many "disabilities." Moreover, the medical profession has added even more labels such as dyslexia, minimal brain damage, perceptual handicaps, and developmental aphasia to the growing list.[23] However, all students are attentive to tasks when they feel successful at them. In reality, we are all differently-abled.

6

Revolutionizing the Curriculum

Inclusive and Earth-Related

A curriculum must be inclusive, life-relevant, and practical and teach stewardship — responsibility — for the earth. We are stewards of the earth. It is our home, it contains our life support system. Our educational curriculum must address it. We have to know how to live in balance with its ecology so we can offer it whole and intact to our children and their children.

Stewardship of the earth involves governing the earth. In Chinese, the word "government" means to put things in the right place, to achieve harmony.[1] The earth puts things in order because it has an order about itself. It is never out of order. It has an adjustable timetable for every eventuality, save one: humankind's possible destruction of it. It knows the doctrine of interdependence, the need to get along with all other bodies in the universe. In a sense the earth has a mind of its own, and the human needs to come under its influence. Robert Muller says:

> Once you find your right, harmonious place in the total order of things, then love, compassion, understanding, good behavior, reverence for life and peaceful relations with others automatically ensue.[2]

The earth actually operates according to the order which Muller mentions about ourselves. This means the earth loves. It not only loves itself, but all creatures it finds placed on it. It means we live in a home where love of self and love of others is the modus operandi of its government. It means that compassion—which means making justice—understanding, and good behavior, which produce cooperation, are also of the very nature of the earth.

We speak today of an earth community because we realize that the earth functions cooperatively. Animals and plants live and work together. The tiniest organisms present in the school yard share a cooperative life-system with all of us. The snail-darter is as important and necessary to life as we are. Mark off just a two meter by two meter square of lawn, and one is looking at a lawn community, where plants and animals live interrelatedly and interdependently. There is a justice about this living, a type of consciousness or understanding which each member of the species has with all the rest of life. When these conditions are present, what Robert Muller says is true: "reverence for life and peaceful relations with others will automatically ensue."

Oftentimes we are poor stewards. We pollute, we rape, we pillage. Brian Swimme asks, "Can earth sustain our violence? Can a great beauty grow from the ruins we leave?"[3] He explains that at one time the earth was able to create life, but that that time has gone because life forms consumed the conditions which allowed that very life to emerge. He believes that the earth will continue on some level, no matter what humans do. However, he tells us that if we continue our chemical and nuclear assault on the planet, future possibilities will be severely limited:

> To expect Rembrandt to create a new painting is fine, but if you first remove an eye and large portions of his brain you will have to accept what he is able to give you out of his diminished capacity.[1]

In our stewardship we need to weave a great tapestry designed by earth itself; a tapestry as different from Galileo, Newton, Copernicus, and Darwin, as night is different from day. As stewards of the earth we have to protect it, learn from it wisely, and allow it to shape us through holy ritual for eons to come. An earth-related, inclusive, and practical curriculum is a must, for it will help us to be both good stewards and develop a new language of living relationships. We can no longer plead ignorance of our effects upon nature, but must be responsible in "the sustaining, renewing, and preserving of the rich diversity of this creation."[5]

An inclusive curriculum is necessary to prepare students to live responsibly and give them a vision of interconnectedness. Robert Muller speaks to this when he says:

> It would be more beneficial to teach children around the world to close their water faucets a few seconds earlier, and to conserve our resources, than to adopt intricate legislation or endlessly drill new holes in the ground.[6]

Much of education has lost sight of the interconnectedness of which Muller speaks. This was evident in the reaction to Sputnik which in the fall of 1957 disturbed the twin sleeping crocodiles of government and education. Once awakened, both flailed around in every direction. In less than a year, in August, 1958, Congress passed the National Defense Education Act which provided loans to college students and financial aid for improving science, mathematics, and modern foreign language instruction.[7] President Kennedy promised to put a man on the moon in ten years. However, years later science curricula were still functioning under a set of conditions similar to its pre-Sputnik times. When asked in 1975 what she thought about the condition of science education, Margaret Mead said, "I hate to think what condition science teaching would be in today if there had been no Sputnik."[8] We can only wonder what the times would have been like had we had an inclusive curriculum many years ago, and had we opted for sharing our scientific knowledge with other countries. Perhaps we could have had joint ventures between the Soviet Union, the United States, and other countries. How much more enriched life on our planet would be if different cultures worked together rather than competed against each other.

Learning should be open to a search for consensus in diversity. "People coalesce in a race, a nation, a language, a religion, a culture, a region, a continent, an alliance, an ideology, a company, a profession . . . ,"[9] says Muller. They feel bound together by these unique collective identities which give them added esteem and the ability for deepening their roots. Without the focus of an inclusive curriculum, groups will continue to behave as if each were the most important one on earth, failing to learn from each other, lacking in compassion and cooperation, failing to realize their collective wisdom. Marilyn Ferguson observes, ". . . no one culture and no period in history has had all the answers." We need the "collective wisdom from the past, and from the whole planet."[10] Teilhard de Chardin believes it is already happening:

> It is almost a commonplace today to find people who, quite naturally and unaffectedly, live in the explicit consciousness of being an atom or a citizen of the universe.[11]

This collective wisdom, these patterns which connect us, so necessary for our continued learning, growth, and humanness, must be nurtured or they will break. Gregory Bateson says, "Break the pattern which connects the items of learning and you necessarily destroy all quality." He goes on to ask, "Why do schools teach almost nothing of the pattern which connects?"[12]

When education perceives itself dualistically as an industry, or narrowly as a type of nationalism, it will not see cultural connecting patterns. Although there is an artist deep within each of us which longs to see through the brokenness of these patterns, schools have to change to recognize and help this inner artist develop. A curriculum needs to have both context and connectedness. "Without context, nothing makes sense,"[13] says Marilyn Ferguson.

A curriculum that is not inclusive in its scope minimizes its context, fails to make connections, and aids and abets fragmentation. The cycle is bound to repeat itself, continuing to market parts for the whole. Furthermore, such a curriculum fails to realize that it contains only a part, and this becomes its epistemological fray. Mary Caroline Richards emphasizes the necessity for interconnectedness in Rudolf Steiner's Waldorf education:

> When a teacher makes a garden with the students, or makes lunch with a class, or shows them how to make a shirt or knit socks, or make a book, or tell a story, or set up a lab experiment, these are part of something real. The garden is part of the earth and related to sun and moon, to weather and seasons, to nourishment of body and soul, to insects and birds and cows and worms, to the mystery and cycle of sprouting and harvesting and seed growing, spring and winter. It is also related to fertility gods and goddesses, to death and resurrection, to myth and poem and play and worship, to history, to science, and to the present community.[14]

Rudolf Steiner also commented on the need for connectedness and wholeness in his schools:

> You see how the important thing for us in our endeavor to achieve teaching that is living rather than dead is always to start from the whole.... We are thus able to place the child in the world in a living way; for the world is a totality and the child maintains permanent links with the living whole.[15]

Erich Jantsch conveys a similar message from a systems science point of view:

> The emergent paradigm of self-organization permits the elaboration of a vision based on the interconnectedness of natural dynamics at all levels of evolving micro- and macrosystems. From such interconnectedness . . . springs a new sense of *meaning*.[16]

Upon reflection, we come to realize that the only world in which we can function is the world which from its creative inception has been whole, dynamic, and self-organizing. We need to fit into that world, care enough to prevent problems, and be compassionate enough to solve the problems we already have. To construct a meaningful future, the human family has to be constantly aware of its roots and its connectedness. Robert Muller says,

> The fulfillment of a human person's earthly destiny, of his happiness during his short life span, of his place in creation, depends in great degree on his comprehension of the total web of life and his personal part and comportment in it.[17]

An inclusive curriculum needs to address this total web of life and enable us to understand and care for peoples of all cultures as well as creatures of space and of the deep. Specifically, an inclusive curriculum would center around a series of investigations embracing the following:[18]

I. Our planetary home and place in the universe

II. The human family

III. Our place in time

IV. The miracle of individual human life

V. Human interactions

VI. Art as meditation

VII. Compassion as a practicum for justice

I. Our Planetary Home and Place in the Universe. This investigation would lead from the infinitely large—the universe—to the infinitely small—atoms, particles, and quarks. It would include the planet earth and our correct place in the universe, our relationship to the stars, outer space, the sun; the earth's physics, climate, atmosphere, biosphere; to seas and oceans, polar ice caps, landmasses, arable lands, deserts, mountains, and water; to plant life, animal life, and human life; to energy, crust, the depths, minerals, microbiolgy, genetics, chemistry, nuclear physics.

Further inquiry would include bioregions: the places where we live. This would look at an examination of the human-earth situation, the possibility of reinhabiting the earth as a new and caring human, and the earth's self-organizing dynamics. It would deal with understanding the transition from homo-centric to bio-centric progress, and understanding the human's participation in a self-propagating, self-nourishing, self-educating, self-governing, self-healing, self-fulfilling, bioregional earth community.

II. The Human Family. This investigation of the quantitative and qualitative characteristics of the human family would include total world population and its changes, human geography and migrations, human longevity, basic races, cultures, and the gifts of people to the planet; sexes, children, youth, adults, the elderly, and the differently-abled. The qualitative characteristics of the human family would include levels of nutrition, health, and standards of life, with definitions of wealth and poverty, skills and employment, education, levels of morality, spirituality, and religion. The investigation of human groupings would include the family, human settlements, professions, corporations, institutions, nations, regions, religions, multinational business, transnational networks, and world organizations.

III. Our Place in Time. This inquiry would include an in-depth look at humanity's place in the dimension of time: past, present, and future. It would investigate ideas about how to preserve the natural elements inherited from the past and necessary for our life and survival (air, water, soils, energy, animals, fauna, flora, genetic materials). It would include our cultural heritage, the landmarks of our evolution and history, and also look into the future to decide how we can hand over to succeeding generations a well-preserved and better-managed planet.

IV. The Miracle of Individual Human Life. This investigation would comprise a study of individual human life as a unique form of universal or divine consciousness — mind — on the planet. It would lead toward correctly seeing institutions, concepts, factories, systems, states, ideologies, and theories, as having no consciousness and therefore existent only as servants and instruments of the increase of human individual consciousness. It would probe the miracle of human life irrespective of race, sex, status, age, nation, or physical or mental capacity. It would look for ways of teaching the art of living and human fulfillment. It would investigate creating ways to make each child feel like a royal person, in kinship and membership with the rest of the created universe.

V. Human Interactions. This investigation would deal with human development, behavior, leadership, and individual and group processes. It would include the policy-making process, compassion as justice, and the healing of the global village. It would investigate leisure in culture, communication for empowerment, self-esteem as a key to well being, educating for critical and corporate consciousness, and world trends.

VI. Art as Meditation. This investigation would be about waking up the inner core of our being, waking up our depths so that our creativity can flow and dance. Thomas Merton speaks of the deep power found in meditation:

> The mind that responds to the intellectual and spiritual values that lie hidden in a poem, a painting, or a piece of music, discovers a spiritual vitality that lifts it above itself, takes it out of itself, and makes it present to itself on a level of being that it did not know it could ever achieve.[19]

The same could be said for what happens to our inner self when we write poetry, photograph a sunset, or create beauty in the flower garden. For art as meditation instills an "attitude of reverence to all existence."[20] It also teaches us about the sacredness of work. Mary Caroline Richards observes:

> There is little reason in our culture to make pottery or furniture or fabric or jewelry by hand except out of an intuitive sense of one's own being and the being of others, and a love for the work.[21]

Art as meditation could be done by anyone in any culture at any time. There are many cultures which have a deep understanding of art as meditation, having practiced it for centuries. Those of us fortunate enough to have strong ethnic roots among parents and grandparents have usually experienced many of its forms: the folk dance, china painting, coloring Easter eggs, playing bocce, etc. It keeps our world from going flat. "It is not a formula we are involved in, but a mystery," says Richards.[22] Art as meditation would enable students to engage in creative movement, helping them to feel at home in their body, recognizing the body's expression and language. It would offer them opportunities to investigate drawing and painting, focusing on their perception of the universe, nature, and the human body. Photography, using the camera in centering and meditation, would show a fuller process of seeing, as well as, in developing and printing, the process of emergence. The experience of playing musical instruments would teach students musical heritage, joy, and delight. Chorus, singing, and songwriting, would befriend both individuals and the earth. Creating rituals for bonding, social transformation, and calling forth energy, would aid in making connections with others and with the earth. Through hatha-yoga, students could learn to befriend their bodies and cherish their breath. Through acupressure they could learn the art of regulating the flow of blood and energy, and experience the innate powers of the body to regulate itself. Through movement, dance, improvisation, and transformation, using mime, clowning, and storytelling, students could experience shaping, delighting, and creating, participating more fully in the creative aspects of the universe. Art as meditation would help students operate from a deeper well of life experiences, see reality more clearly, and be open to truth in a more radical way.

VII. Compassion as a Practicum for Justice. Matthew Fox tells us that compassion comes from the Latin "cum patior," "meaning to suffer with, to undergo with, to share solidarity with."[23] A practicum for justice would enable students to learn first-hand how other human beings function, live, hope, interact, and die. It would awaken students to the interdependencies of creation, the threats to our global village, the violence of nature and of people, and the power, found deep within the human race, to create alternatives to the problems faced by our world and planet. What Fox says of economics could be said of compassion as a practicum for justice:

REVOLUTIONIZING THE CURRICULUM

Do not tell us whether our economy is growing in Gross National Product yearly: rather tell us whether our world-wide economics are accomplishing the following: housing for the homeless, feeding the hungry, educating the ignorant, caring for the sick, humanizing the prisons, creating good work for the unemployed, encouraging technology with a human face, celebrating with the forgotten, passing on nature's energies to other generations.[24]

Students could put forth an enormous energy in compassion for their fellow human beings and for the befriending of the planet. An internship should be designed to give students a hands-on experience in different areas of social change. For example, students in sixth to eighth grades could do apprentice work while older students from high school could take on leadership and work roles. Students and teachers could engage in any of the following programs that appealed to them or work to create their own.

1. Residential Health Care for Senior Citizens. Students would experience working with senior citizens in health care, nutrition education, self-esteem, and problems of identity among the aged. They could help to organize a program of day trips and nighttime experiences for the homebound, and have daily interchange between senior citizens and themselves.

2. Weekends in the Neighborhood Programs. Student groups would celebrate the gifts of the people in mime, storytelling, music, dance, juggling, poetry, dramatic reading, art, folk dancing, pottery, and creative movement. Students would help to organize neighborhood events, including themes with chorus, street drama, and music. They would reach out to others through massage, creating rituals, clowning, games, and neighborhood cookouts sponsored by neighbors; and through crafts, art, movies in the streets, and street dances.

3. Rehabilitation of Housing. Students would perform work in all phases and processes of home rehabilitation: planning, carpentry, plumbing, electrical, plastering, painting and decorating; cement repairs and landscaping. Through their caring, blighted neighborhoods would be renewed.

4. Cooperative Gardening and Farm Stands. Applying their learning from school gardens, students would aid residents, particularly senior citizens, in preparing land, seeding, and harvesting. They would help organize the program with families and help sell produce at the farm stand.

5. Community Choruses. Students would aid in developing a chorus and band to compose, sing, and play all styles of music, travel from community to community, and aid members in beginning other choruses where invited.

6. Performing Arts Groups. Students would aid in developing drama groups sponsored by businesses whose members would perform original and professional plays in neighborhoods.

7. Handyperson Programs. Students would aid in developing their talents to do work for the poor, the elderly, and those who simply could not do a job that needs to be done. Students would also learn the art of negotiating, setting prices, and bartering. Their work would include electrical wiring, painting, plumbing, cleanup, washing windows, masonry, and carpentry.

8. Day Care and Parenting Centers. Students would aid in operating day care centers for infants and children, and help out in elder care centers for senior citizens. Teachers and students could organize and hold parenting sessions, using programs like *Systematic Training for Effective Parenting*.[25]

9. Universities of the Streets. Students would aid in surveying neighborhoods and determining needs for educational outreach in communities. Working with educational institutions, interested businesses, merchants, and residents, they would help organize classes and degree courses for a personal growth academy. This academy would include courses in any area people wished to learn, as well as in neighborhood organizing and empowerment, assertiveness, self-esteem, parenting, beginning relationships, ending relationships, divorce, compassion, and celebration.

REVOLUTIONIZING THE CURRICULUM

Robert Muller tells us that education must give students a correct view of reality if we want our children to have an honest view of the world:

> We must give them a global view of the planet's marvels and conditions, of the human family and its rich diversity, we must give them to understand that they are a cosmos of their own endowed with the miracle of life among innumerable brethren and sisters on our planet.[26]

This practicum for justice would help educators, students, and parents find their center, the center from which experience, growth, and maturity take place. It would help them develop meaning in their lives, help them feel connected to the earth, effectively eliminate boredom, and help them to design and create jobs that make sense and have purpose.

Stimulating Young Children and Adolescents

Educators and parents frequently say that children and adolescents are lazy, that they are people who do not want to learn. Nothing could be further from the truth. Educators and parents need to understand how human beings grow and develop, and they need to work to rid themselves of defeatist beliefs and to rid the systems of education of deficiencies — this is where the difficulties lie. Children and adolescents come to the schools ready to be challenged, and too often, they are told to sit in an assigned chair, stay there for most of the day, do assigned work, and speak only when they are spoken to. Under these circumstances stimulation becomes replaced by frustration, and ultimately, boredom.

Learning and Young Children

Education is an art. Its artistry lies in its ability to deal with temperaments and creative rhythms in every phase of a child's life. These rhythms must consistently call forth appropriate responses on the part of teachers and educators. In young children especially, teaching must appeal to their feelings rather than try to impart information via the intellect. Ernst Buhler calls children's feelings "their character-building forces."[27] These character-building forces develop over many years as children of all temperaments feel loved, as educators stress the dignity and individuality of each child, and adapt their teaching methods to all phases of a child's development from kindergarten through high school. René M. Querido calls the education of children a "truly holistic pedagogy, one that encompasses education of the heart, hand, and mind."[28] The order that he mentions is important. Too often American education stresses the hand in kindergarten and the mind from first grade through twelfth grade. Rarely are matters of the heart brought into the classroom. Very young children need to be fascinated by the wonders of nature which they sense all around them. Children need to be given the experience of form, color, and language, because these strengthen the elemental creative forces and allow them to unfold in a more emotionally healthy way. This is the reason everything should be done as creatively and artistically as possible. In the later grades balance emerges from participation in the artistic and the practical academic activities.

During the first seven years of life children learn principally by imitation. Up to age six or seven children mimic uncritically everything in the environment, not only the sounds of speech, the gestures of people and machines, but the attitudes and values of parents and peers.[29]

After age seven, children develop a vivid life of imagination and exhibit a readiness for more formal learning. Young children particularly delight in singing, dressing up, movement, acting, and making music with rhythm instruments. They like storytelling which eases them into form and letter drawing, which are important at this stage because they are fundamental to reading. Rudolf Steiner believes that reading is a process which begins with the "living word" in the form of a teacher telling a story. Children listening to stories develop vigorous mental pictures which are inherent to the reading process. Then, in drawing lessons, the teacher introduces another "language," the language of form. Here the shape of letters emerge from the connection between mental images and particular forms. Later, through the recitation of drama, or some other form of language, *the child* speaks, and the letters which have been learned are used to write down this already spoken content. The final step is "to read" the classroom library, following these initial stages.[30]

Music, movement, handwork, and languages should be taught early when children excel in their capacity to mimic. It is then that they will learn accents which will help them speak languages fluently. Learning correct grammar comes at a later time, and is easily inserted into the language flow. Also later, come such subjects as gymnastics, woodworking, and gardening. All these aid in building awareness of a strong individuality, which nurtures the seeds for the later concepts of freedom and responsibility.

Educational curricula must offer the full breadth of experience to children so that as they grow and approach adulthood they will have the knowledge, skills, and interests to make meaningful decisions for their lives. "The *hand* must learn to cook, sew, knit, bind books, and master other crafts," says Querido.[31] Young children learn coordination in movement, learn grace through gestures and touch, learn proper breathing and appreciate the beauty of their bodies through gymnastics. They must also be taught how their hands can heal. Through the hand comes the awakening and learning of the doing part of our personality. Through the activity of the hand comes drawing and writing and integrating stories heard and told.

Then comes the activity of the heart. Through the heart students are touched very deeply; their hearts capture imagination and feelings. When hearts are touched, learning becomes alive, electric. "Is Pythagoras simply a name that is connected with a rather tiresome theorem about a hypotenuse and the squares of two sides?"[32] asks Querido. Students need to learn about Pythagoras the human being. When students identify with his life, struggles, joys, and sorrows, they come to appreciate and see the importance of his discoveries. The desire to know more about him and his theories is awakened. Getting to know the person and how he or she developed famous theories removes the pressure from learning. When children are educated this way they learn not only facts and ideas, but they learn to connect them to everyday experiences. When they learn about the humanness of famous people, they live with less pressure themselves because they get to know about these people on another level. They know about the pain, suffering, and endurance of Pythagoras; they know about the one hundred thousand tries by a determined Edison to make an electric lamp; about the painful headaches that Pascal had because the soft spot on top of his head never closed and how studying math and geometry helped him overcome the pain.

The heart is *the* way to gain entry to students. It is their hearts which open them in geography to know personally the people of Russia, how they deal with the long, cold winters, how they cook their food, what foods they prefer, what they do for leisure, how they celebrate their festivals, and how they think and relate with others. They want to know as personally as possible the people of Germany, of Scandinavia, of Iceland, of South Africa, of Mexico, of Venezuela, Peru, and Chile. Knowledge through the heart allows students to *experience* for themselves the oneness of the earth and their oneness with it.

Without the hand and the heart there is no connection with the head. The way to the head comes through the hand and the heart. When it does not come this way, facts and other data become vacuous, an intellectual abstraction which is deadening to a child. "A child cannot relate to it: it is foreign to the joy and sorrow of his or her everyday life," says Querido.[33] So it is that the child is brought to abstraction gradually, through the involvement of immediate feelings, through making connections with reality. This is usually done when students are in about the eighth or ninth grade, when they can gradually be introduced to science and technology. This means that educators must be willing to change their whole modus operandi so that the curriculum can be seen in its truest sense, namely, responding to where children are at in *their* development. It is simply *wrong* to try to force development of the intellect before it is ready. Educators and parents must shun publishers, entrepreneurs, and "specialists," who market flash cards and reading programs for three-year-olds, and hawk their "scientific studies" which place measurement over and against development.

Educators must be strong in their desire to ensure that the environment is safe. A. S. Neill says he would not have American horror comics in his school. "I don't think it's fair for a small child to be faced with all that perversity and sickness that we call humor, made by sick men — mind you — perverted men."[34] Children who will imitate *everything* must have school environments *worthy* of imitation; spaces of continual caring where they can

REVOLUTIONIZING THE CURRICULUM

develop in a gradual, easy, safe, and loving way. Young children, especially, have an antenna-like ability to pick up and drink in the environment. They trust implicitly; they are remarkably sensitive—they imitate not only what is being done but what is being felt. They also are remarkably vulnerable and need to be protected. They cannot be turned loose on their own in a laissez-faire atmosphere nor can they be programmed like a computer. Hence, parents and teachers are charged with creating an environment which is both highly stimulating and worthwhile. Some questions should be asked. Outside of a few children's television shows, such as Mr. Rogers' Neighborhood, Sesame Street, and Captain Kangaroo, are television, put-down comic books, commercials, cigarette smoke, alcohol abuse, communication through yelling, harsh words, and screaming radios, worthy of imitation? We have been paying a steep price in every way by being blasé about the environment in which we place children, in insisting on early specialization, and in treating children as if they were little adults or little teenagers. Not only have we been robbing them of their childhood, but we have been replacing it with our own neurotic creations. Our children are precious, and their education must be a sacred trust.

Learning and Adolescents

The "truly holistic pedagogy" of which Querido speaks must also be available to adolescents. Society's demands of dualism, dichotomizing, and compartmentalizing education, which pressures teenagers so much it is literally killing them, is really a denial of the growth and maturing process. The hand, the heart, and the head must be the pathways to learning in adolescence and adulthood too. After puberty the thinking power and capacity for judgment need an outlet for action. So the environment for adolescent students is different from that of younger students but no less important. They need an environment proportionate in freedom and responsibility, one which will allow them to use and hone their skills of reason and logic. They need to try things on their own, but not completely. Caring teachers who are listeners must be available for teenagers to "check things out" with them. Some family teachers and guidance counselors fulfill this function of being expert listeners, but many educators need to become better listeners—people who hear without making judgments.

Adolescents are in constant contact with all of life, especially the practical; that is where they receive stimulation. At this stage many traditional teachers feel that students need to be held down. The opposite is the real adolescent need. Teenagers need to be allowed to look beneath every rock, to ask every kind of question, to search for alternatives, to ponder every kind of human problem. They are at an age which is rich in riddles and surprises, where feelings run deep, enthusiasm runs high, and the mastery of consciousness occurs slowly. Rudolf Steiner says that during these teenage years, teachers must consistently give lessons with imagination, enthusiasm, and artistic feeling.[35]

It is also important that students after puberty begin to receive their lessons from a number of specialist teachers, and that they begin to think of these teachers as heroes and mentors. The importance of this should not be overlooked. Adolescents want and need adults with whom they establish a bond of trust in a different way from when they were youngsters. They want to be "in charge" of picking and choosing those whom they relate to; they want to do everything "now," and they want to use the trial and error method for their successes and failures. Having been taught consequences for actions early in life, they are more than willing to make new choices based on them. This process allows them to learn valuable lessons about relationships which they will apply as they "fall in love," and later, as they begin thinking about taking deeper relational risks. Seven-to-twelve-year-olds expect adults to know everything, and, in a way, teenagers still hope for this, but now their expectations will lead them in the gradual understanding that they are becoming their own authority. It is this understanding that will allow them to realize their own authority over themselves as adults. Hence, the role of the secondary school teacher must be clearly seen. He or she needs to be perceived as a master of his or her subject; as a master who is willing to teach students and learn from them, and be that rare kind of guide who is there to listen and be able to step out of the way when adolescents try their wings.

The successful secondary school should make available the broadest possible curriculum. Students need not take everything that is offered, but schools should be a type of supermarket of offerings. Schools need to be a "both/and," allowing students the freedom to gravitate towards chosen people and areas of activity according to their taste and talents, and yet offer structure in such a way that students will want to accept the disciplines of many subjects. In this way students can come to appreciate the illumination and mutual support that comes from an interdisciplinary approach, seeing school and themselves as a living microcosm in the living macrocosm of the world.

Schools need this "best of both worlds" approach. They could offer structured classes, building on the foundations students received in elementary school. They could offer peer-matching, finding a person who would serve as a teacher in any conceivable discipline. This teacher could be anyone who has a desire to impart a skill students wished to learn. The teacher need not be certified. A peer-match teacher may be a neighbor fluent in Spanish, a cook in a restaurant, a salesperson, an electrician, etc. In peer-matching, the teacher search itself would be an educational experience. Through networking and peer-matching, schools can put students and teachers into contact with each other. This is an exciting approach to education. Ivan Illich says that "peer-matching facilities should be available for individuals who want to bring people together as easily as the village bell called the villagers to a council."[36] He says further:

> If a student wanted to learn spoken Cantonese from a Chinese neighbor, the pedagogue would be available to judge their proficiency, and to help them select the textbook and methods most suitable to their talents, character, and the time available for study.[37]

Obviously, peer-matching could be done with every subject on every grade level in high school. It would require changes in the thinking of administrators and teachers, from a more traditional to a more entrepreneurial educational concept, but networks which would emerge would be rich sources of further education. This would ease many of the burdens educators presently face.

The following curriculum suggestions apply both to the structured classroom and to the learning web which comes about through networking. In using either method or some combination of both methods, students should have an opportunity to develop a curriculum which reflects their own desires as well as the desires of parents and educators. This suggested curriculum offers a starting place for schools to look creatively at curriculum possibilities.

In literature, for example, students should approach the aesthetic problems, and as they move into higher grades, begin to see their own development as a microcosm of the world-development macrocosm. Any reading should foster conclusions about the present day world. By the junior year in high school, literature should become the history books for students. They should be able to understand that in the Middle Ages the moral and physical realms were perceived as a unity and how and why this perception was lost in the 15th and 16th centuries. They should understand the difference between lay and clerical education in the Middle Ages.[38] In his Waldorf curriculum, Rudolf Steiner asks for teachers who know a great deal about the interrelatedness of history and life and how literature reflected this: "The teacher needs to show how at the end of the 19th century the spiritual heritage of past ages dwindles away and how all traditions become gradually thinner until nothing remains but a mere thread."[39]

In science, students need to understand how nature is classified according to abstract laws by the intellect, and they need to begin to understand how cause and effect are connected in individual instances in physics. They need to grasp the concepts behind mechanics, electricity, telegraphy and satellite transmission, X-rays, radio activity, and silicon computer chips. Adolescents need to comprehend optics and technology, as well as economics and labor practices which come about from discovery and invention. Study in the natural and social sciences, from anthropology to psychology, from chemistry to zoology, must be available to students, all taught from the basis and relevance of human and other life relationships. In the study of the cell, for example, pupils should be aware of the great cosmic relationships which are mirrored even in the smallest substances, for when cells divide they repeat the primeval cosmic activities from which they, the pupils, have their being.[40] A thorough grounding in biology, with emphasis on the plant and animal kingdoms, should be understood as well. Organic and inorganic chemistry, the chemical phenomena in living organisms, chemical processes, and substances, need to be seen in light of human purpose and stewardship on earth.

With this understanding must come balance, and that balance is achieved in the feeling for art and the various arts which have developed over human history. Without this balance students' right brains will be deprived while their left brains become favored, thereby missing "whole brain" integration. The concepts of beauty, art for "art's sake," and the transition of art through different times, can help students find answers to problems they are facing at this stage of their growth and development. Poetry as art, language as artistic medium, and artistic speech needs to become as a living being in the hearts of students. Through listening to Goethe's language, students should feel the stirrings of their own personal transformations taking place. Teachers need to show how the spiritual life of the country is nourished by its music, poetry, and painting. As students study history, they will make connections with a people's art and begin to see differences in cultural worldviews. As they become familiar with folk art around the world, they will see it as a particular expression of a people at a given moment. They should become familiar with forms and styles of the great cultural epochs of history and understand the changes brought about when traditional styles gave way to new ideas of such things as reinforced concrete, plastic, and fiberglass. Steiner has specific advice for how teachers present the ideas of art:

> The teacher should create in the pupils the feeling that neither the single human being nor the life of the whole community can be truly healthy if their creative artistic powers cannot find the right expression.[11]

He says further, referring to students in their senior year: "As a conclusion to their [high] school life the pupils should be awakened to an appreciation of the realm of the beautiful which is also the realm of freedom . . . ."[42] When the artist has been awakened in every student there will be a renaissance of aesthetics in our country which will enable us to understand more deeply the native peoples of our land, and bring us into harmony with the earth.

In history, students should learn to understand the character and times of the epoch into which they are born. Inner historical motives should be presented so that students begin to compare, for example, state alliances with the older social alliances of the 16th and 17th centuries, and with social alliances they themselves are forming among their peers. Students should know how peoples of the world are all dependent on the same earth and climate for their living. They should be familiar with the lives of historical people from Eastern and Greek history, and know why there was a decline in freedom in the Grecian states under Alexander the Great. They should know how a people change when historical events force them to change their environment. By the time students are in their senior year, they should comprehend that historical events are part of the whole evolutionary process, connected to all life of which they are vital parts. Students should understand their own place in present developments and sense their *responsibility* for what is going on in the world.

In geography, students should learn of the structure of mountain divisions and their own connections with these divisions over the whole earth. The earth and its grandeur, its changes, its toughness and fragility, should be described both structurally and physically as a whole. Students should understand land surveying, world geography, and mapmaking.

In mathematics, exercises in thinking out problems — combinations, variations, linear equations, the binomial theorem — should be given. Students should be introduced to logarithms in algebra, trigonometrical functions, and plane and spherical geometry. Mathematical work should be applied to astronomy, nautical triangles, and architecture.

In language, students should study to develop a deeper understanding of the life patterns of other peoples and their cultures. Steiner says that "the reading of the language is of chief importance," and that understanding should be gained by "explanations in the foreign language, and by suitable retelling and free conversations about problems."[43] In this too, the retelling of problems allows students to develop insight and ultimately master their own problems. Latin and Greek studies will come alive as students read Caesar and learn the poems of Ovid, Virgil, and easier passages of Cicero. These readings will serve to introduce students to the worldview of that time. There is a natural connection for students between understanding languages and dramatic presentations. French and German classical drama should be studied and performed giving special attention to the beauty of the language.[44] Readings from *The Odyssey* and the easier dialogues of Plato can also be dramatized. By students' senior year they should be reading present day literature in each of the languages. Thus will they heighten their awareness of the soul of these cultures. In Latin and Greek especially, students will have developed an introduction to philosophy which will enrich them throughout life. Study of classical languages will whet their appetites for study of other languages, especially those of the East, Japanese and Chinese.

In physics, students should understand heat and mechanics and their role in the locomotive. In the same way, they should study electricity, magnetism, and sound, and their role in the telephone. These provided the chief means of electronic communication, the precursor to radio, television, satellite communications, and fiber optics.

In movement and dance, adolescents sense the connection between their bodies and what they are taking in via their senses and mind. The surge of energy which developed from various personal and state relationships during different historical epochs parallels adolescent surges of energy. These adolescent surges are discharged most effectively in movement classes where students dance poetry, history lessons, geography, literature, science, and music. As Steiner says, ". . . something becomes visible which usually remains only audible."[45] By their senior year, students should be able to dance so that the rhythms of the solar system are manifested. Other rhythms find expression in music. Singing in a mixed choir for all secondary school students allows them to focus energy and promote delights for all creation. Playing a musical instrument of their choice and training them in musical literature with an eye towards understanding music as an historical response, fosters their understanding of aesthetics. Learning to compose and perform their own melodies in class and in the community teaches self-confidence and the power of art.

Handwork is especially important for adolescents because their design capabilities and the products they create build their esteem, give them a creative outlet, and help them make meaning in life. This meaning is increased as their creations are made available for parents, siblings, relatives, friends, and the marketplace. Cushions, clothes, hats, sweaters, baskets, embroidery, portfolios, photo albums, wallets, paintings, posters, books bound and gilded, as well as clay, stone, and wood sculptures, and other works of art, teach adolescents the value of time spent in a leisurely way, and the satisfaction gained from making something by hand.

In gymnastics, adolescents channel their energies while developing all systems of the body. Jumping, swinging, running, walking, learning how to fall, doing flips, rolls, tumbling, ball throwing, and aerobics, help adolescents tone their bodies, enrich their minds, and enliven their spirits. These exercises strengthen adolescent students for track and field sports and help them sharpen their judgmental skills. This will have positive effects on much of their later endeavors, from driver education to life decisions. It also places them in rhythm with the earth which also moves, jumps, tumbles, and breathes.

Through the careful education of their first eight years, adolescents gain considerable understanding of the earth and their connections with it. In gardening, they have the opportunity directly to sense these connections in the cycles of birth, life, and death. The wintertime, when everything appears to be dormant, is a ripe time for undertaking theoretical lessons in gardening. Students learn about shrubs and trees, the cultivation and care of annual plants, grafting of fruit and other trees, and the methods of approaching the land with reverence. They need to study land preparation, how to plant a vegetable garden, crop rotation, and methods of planting and tending. Math skills, social skills, knowledge of history and geography, and more, come into play in the garden. "Give and take" gets learned as teachers help students work out a program for summer caring of the garden. Decisions will have to be made about harvesting and how the harvest will be shared. The garden not only will yield fruit and vegetables, but will give impetus to rituals and festivals, thereby further connecting education and living.

There is no end to curriculum subjects which can be offered in and through the high school that cares. Certainly first aid, business skills, advanced typing, and computers, need to be available, and education in sexuality should be continued from the early grades. Everything taught should be done so from a living worldview. Dull lectures, passivity, and textbooks written without imagination, have no place in any school. There is a rhythm and excitement in students after puberty. High schools need to be places of both wild activity and corners of solitude, with horns going off when mistakes are made so that passersby will know that learning is taking place.

Learning from the School of Life

There is a powerful story told by Harrison Salisbury, noted *New York Times* writer and author, about one of his ancestors named Hiram Salisbury and how he was a "man of his time," 1815. Harrison Salisbury tells us that Hiram knew every farm chore, that he milked cows and attended calves in birth, cultivated the earth and grafted fruit trees, made cider and built cider mills. He butchered the hogs, sheared the sheep, churned butter, made soap and candles, thatched barns, and built smokehouses. He fought forest fires, built furniture and wagons, made house frames and beams, fixed clocks, and found time for fishing. He carved board measures — a type of yardstick — and sold them for a dollar apiece. He ran a bookstore and made coffins. He was a member of the state's General Assembly, overseer of the poor, appraiser of property, and fellow of the town council. "I do not think he was an unusual man," says Harrison Salisbury.

> Put me in Hiram's world and I would not last long. Put Hiram down in our world, he might have a little trouble with a computer, but he'd get the hang of it faster than I could cradle a bushel of oats.[46]

Salisbury's story is penetrating. It teaches us that life is full of learning. To learn we have to be engaged in *living* life, not just satisfied with a laundered version, trivialized, sterilized, and packaged. Brian Swimme speaks to this point when he says: "You will know when you fail to learn, for failure is punished with boredom."[47] One could wager a bet that Hiram Salisbury was never bored. He may not have liked something going on in his life, he may have grumbled at hard work, he may have wished he had more sunlight in his days, but it is doubtful that he was bored. It is hard to find boredom in anyone who lives adventurously, anyone who is enthralled with living.

Hiram Salisburies are still around today. People who know deep in their bones that life is the teacher *par excellence*. Many of them are seriously questioning present public education. Some of them have taken their children out of formal schooling, or are not sending them to begin with, letting life be their curriculum. Their numbers are growing and their stories are significant. In *Teach Your Own,* John Holt tells some of their stories.

A teenager who has been without formal schooling for two years said, "I learned how to live without grades and not to need someone to tell me 'It's good' every time I did something . . . ." He went on to say that public schools do not offer *experience* and that he relates better now with adults because he is around them more. "I am capable of doing so many more things it amazes me. And it's all because I had the time to learn, and enjoy while I was learning."[48]

A father told of the experiences of two of his children in "lifeschool" when they moved to a farm. Although his daughter was twelve, she pitched in as an adult, learning from experience. When she was thirteen the family went to help another commune with sugaring, and she "fell in love with the place," even though it meant using primitive and horse-drawn equipment. She asked to stay and has lived there for over five years.

After she came home she wanted to apply for a government vocational program. Because she needed a high school diploma she went to an adult education class for a few months and took the test. She passed in the top percentile, was offered scholarships to various colleges, and "graduated" earlier than her classmates who stayed in school. "I think her case illustrates especially dramatically the waste of time in schools," said her father. He went on to say that between the ages of thirteen and eighteen, she moved comfortably into womanhood and acquired a vast number of skills. She had a vast range of experiences in the adult world, and still qualified exceptionally by academic standards. Her classmates who stayed in school were in many cases "stunted in mind, emotionally disturbed, without significant goals or directions or sound values in their lives."[49]

This father also spoke of his younger child, a son named Topher, who learned simply by following adults around, by helping and asking questions — becoming involved. By age eight he had amassed an impressive array of skills: baking bread and cakes, repairing machines, and wiring lamps and rooms. He had a considerable knowledge of automobiles, calculators, tape recorders and videotape equipment. He knew the usual farm tasks such as gardening, animal care, foresting, wildlife, and rocks. His father noted that he has always had a strong interest in geology and electronics, weather, and machines of all kinds. "He helped us at many tasks in our small factory, manufacturing planters from small oak logs."[50]

A mother, who with her husband and three sons moved to an island off the coast of Maine, told about her children learning to dig clams in extremely cold weather with the "clammers of Maine, the salt of the earth." They learned to take responsibility for each other's lives. The family listened to the radio and they all came to like and understand opera. They learned to make value decisions when, of the eight unexpected puppies born, five had to be destroyed because of the food shortage. They learned how to get along with themselves and each other.

She said the family could read books until 1 A.M. because no one had to be up for the school bus. Because of their reading, they were exposed to the history, literature, mythology, and architecture of Greece and decided to take a trip there:

> . . . a trip we would never have been interested in taking or felt a need to take if 'doors' hadn't been opened for us. Bud came to love the Parthenon and had to see it. Tim was a walking encyclopedia on mythology and gave Jack and me the tour in the Archaeological Museum, and Mike was our history guide — we didn't even need a Greek service.[51]

A cover story of the April, 1980, issue of *Home Educators Newsletter,* told about Katrina, who spends several hours morning and afternoon doing farm work, keeps all the records for feed, hay, and other purchases to calculate her profit when animals are sold, and figures what work-hours and money have been expended to gain that profit. The author of the article was quite astonished at her capabilities:

> How much barley will a pig eat in a week, a month, till time for the market? What animals have the quickest turnover? What type of labor hours are necessary to operate a farm? I couldn't answer any of these questions, though Katrina can, and for an eleven-year-old girl I consider that quite an accomplishment.[52]

In addition to her farm work, she does a reading assignment of 200 pages per week, and a written paper every day.

TRANSFORMING EDUCATION

Katrina's parents said they are presently sectioning off a room in the basement, and all the partitions will be built by the children. John, who is seven, has all his own tools, including a power saw and drill. He will be in charge of measuring and cutting boards for the partition project and is also planning on paneling his own room.

The family dishwasher has been child-repaired, the bathroom child paneled, toilets child-plumbed. One son built his own motorized three-wheel all-terrain vehicle, and helped his dad build a one-man plane. He has developed one patent and is working on another.

The parents said they would have no qualms about letting their thirteen-year-old plumb the entire house. After all, "he wired it . . . when he was only eight."[53] Daughter Cathy, at nineteen, is remodeling her own home: doing all the plumbing, plastering, wallpapering, and carpentry. She helped pay for her college education by working as a carpenter in an all-male shop.

A mother spoke about her children and money:

> Heidi and Michael have just bought themselves ponies with their own money . . . . Heidi (10) wrote a cheque for hers.
> I don't know what other banking practices are like, but at our credit union any child can have a full-fledged account (and *must* be a shareholder in the corporation in order to have an account).[54]

Children are alive with enthusiasm, open to exploration, eager to probe. If schools are going to be places where education happens, they must meet these challenging children with access to the laboratory that is life. Often American education is so locked into the status quo that it ceases to be stimulating and innovating. Neil Postman and Charles Weingartner comment on education's malaise:

> Basically, the structure of a conventional school requires that everyone be there when the school is ready, that everyone learn what the school teaches *when* it teaches it, and *where* it teaches it — all together, at the same time and in the same place. This is simply not the way human beings learn — anything.[55]

Education must end its arrogance. Schools can learn much from those who were and are life-taught. Salisbury's ancestor certainly achieved much and could teach much. John Holt asks where

Hiram Salisbury learned all those skills and suggests, "Not in school, nor in workshops or any other school-like activity."[56] He mentions the importance of valuing children, and the importance of the adult-child relationship, and what Hiram Salisbury learned from it: "Almost certainly, he learned how to do all those kinds of work, many of them highly skilled, by being around when other people were doing them. But these people were not doing the work in order to teach Hiram something . . . . They said, 'Hiram, I'm raising a barn and *I need your help.*' He was there to help, not to learn—but as he helped, he learned."[57]

In every one of the above stories, the people in them felt needed. Their ideas were needed, their skills were needed; they were needed. Because they were needed, they were valued; counted rather than discounted. These individuals explored what they wanted to, delved deeply, questioned any and every authority they could find, read far into the night, made moves in their lives that enhanced their esteem—in short, they educated themselves according to their own time table and interests.

Unfortunately, exploration and discovery have not accrued for most of their counterparts enrolled in traditional schooling. In the traditional school setting few know the joy that is the school of life, with its varied and wonderful curriculum which opens rather than closes doors, which respects dreams, which touches the artist deep within, which aids in the development of leadership skills and enhances the sense of responsibility. Why is this so? Pick up most curriculum materials today and the sense instantly communicated is one of dominance, of control, estrangement, and alienation. The graphics on the front cover of the recently published study, *Effective Schools and Classrooms: A Research-Based Perspective,* authored by the Association for Supervision and Curriculum Development, depict children and adults in small boxes, boxes supposed one guesses, to represent classrooms.[58] This is no mistake, as reading the book points out quite clearly. These researchers see education's job as doing whatever it takes to get students to amass a certain content of "knowledge" and pass tests so that the schools can look good. As one principal points out in an interview: "When teachers agree on what all students should learn, then student achievement is likely to improve and everyone is more likely to succeed."[59] This presupposes that any information, knowledge, ideas, and creativity students come with will be discounted — at least in this school — unless it fits into this principal's idea of a curriculum. Educators buying the research in this book — it was partially funded by the National Institute of Education — will wreak havoc and have damaging effects on their schools and students. Consider the statement that "Student achievement can be measured with validity and reliability in important areas."[60] Some serious questions have to be asked: What does achievement mean? What is the purpose of the measurement? What are "important areas"? If it is possible to measure student achievement — and this is questionable — why is it necessary? Most daily newspapers tell the stories of what happens to children when we force them into the boxes in which researchers want them to function.

Another statement spells out even more clearly the goals of these researchers: "When teachers teach most of the content and skills covered by standardized tests, students are likely to have higher achievement scores."[61] Of course. But what happens to the inner and outer life of students when this goes on? What about the real meaning of *"educare"*? Where is the "drawing out"? Where is the wonder? What connections get made? Where is the joy? Where is the critical questioning? Where is the possibility of transformation?

7

Transforming Leadership

Lessons from the Best-Run Companies

Leadership plays a significant role in every organization. It offers direction, gets people acting, gets them to believe in themselves and in what they are doing, and helps them get excited about their learning. In education especially, leadership needs to be creative, innovative, and upbeat. Leaders need to lead, and to lead excellently. They need to sense the needs of their followers and they need to help these followers become transformed. In so doing they will be open to their own transformation. They will do what Paulo Freire deems most essential for educators: they will reverse roles and become students themselves. Marilyn Ferguson reminds us that "Transforming leadership cannot be a one-way street."[1] Educational leaders who realize this will be adept in their dual roles: being transforming leaders and full-time, excellent students. They will validate what James MacGregor Burns says: "True leadership not only helps satisfy our present needs. . . . It awakens us to deeper dissatisfactions, hungers";[2] or as Marilyn Ferguson says further: *"The true leader fosters a paradigm shift in those who are ready."* [3]

American students are waiting to have their consciousness aroused. Perhaps never before has there been such a sleeping giant ready to help society transform. Students need to be made ready for the paradigm shift. They need to be made aware of the importance of reaching critical mass, of the significance of the present times, and of the synchronicities of world events, so that the breakthrough which is on the horizon can bring to birth the new human.

Transforming leaders in education will play a deeply personal role in effecting this breakthrough for they know that the energy that flows in their bodies and spirits allows them to risk a new kind of leadership. They will not be afraid to prune away those who have not been effective either because they did not have leadership skills to begin with, or because they lost them along the way due to a lack of consistent development. Transforming leaders in education will be more sure of their roles. They will not be playing it safe, hiding behind budget cuts, or blaming school boards who "tie our hands." In their book about best-run companies, Thomas J. Peters and Robert H. Waterman, Jr. talk about this transforming kind of leadership:

> Only if you want to get people *acting* even in small ways, the way you want them to, will they come to believe in what they're doing. . . . "Doing things" (lots of experiments, tries) leads to rapid and effective learning, adaptation, diffusion, and commitment; it is the hallmark of the well-run company.[4]

Getting people acting applies to all educators, from school boards to superintendents, from principals to classroom teachers, their support staff, and parents. If educators cannot get students, parents, taxpayers, and the community acting in favor of the real meaning of education, if they cannot get them excited about all learning, then they are offering *wrong* ideas in their leadership. Acting "even in small ways, the way you want them to," means that trust is so much a characteristic of leadership that the group will want to enter into the leader's *vision,* will want to follow the thrust of the leader's direction, will want to cooperate, and, in the words of Lao-tse, will say, "We did it ourselves." Leadership is not coercion, which is force and lasts only as long as the force is held in place; it is the announcement of a vision and it is people catching the vision, willingly exploring it in a group united for mutual benefit, and giving and receiving feedback. It is realizing "the truth of Thoreau's injunction: *Live* your beliefs, and you can turn the world around."[5]

Some may think shared vision, trust, and frequent interaction would never work in education. "You'll never get parents working together with you. Oh, a few of them, yes, but never all of them." "You don't understand about school boards; they're voted in by popularity and sometimes because of a vendetta, not by what they know of the educational process." "The Central Office doesn't give me any support." "It's the superintendent," or "the principal," or "the teachers," or "the parents." When leaders fall into these pits of negativity and erroneous beliefs, they doubt their own ability to lead, they lose sight of their vision and ideals, and they lead poorly.

Much can be learned about leadership and management in the schools by looking at the best-run companies in business. Some might say schools are different, which, certainly is true. Others might say that even the best-run companies have been guilty of exploiting, polluting, and falling into and perpetuating other pathologies; this also is true. But the ability for these best-run companies to sense and respond to customers and stock holders, to recognize problems, and either voluntarily or through public outcry, address them, can be helpful to educators. Transforming leadership must sense what John Naisbitt speaks of in *Megatrends:* "Followers create leaders. Period."[6] He says further that, "The new leader is a facilitator, not an order giver."[7] These statements are true in the best-run companies. What these best-run companies can contribute to education is their approach to leadership. The style of leadership, the techniques, the ability of leaders to share their company vision and build it into a philosophy which the workers believe in and therefore want to follow — that kind of cooperation and the level of trust necessary for it, are the same in the best-run companies and in systems of education.

Educational opportunities in the company are hands-on, with people acting through story, role play, drama, and fieldwork. Their students study together and on their own. They are encouraged to create new and farther-reaching ideas. Materials are clear, lean, and extremely current, usually photocopied papers in 3-ring binders, with graphs and charts very capable of being changed, dropped, or added.

These workers and trainees believe in what they are doing, and they frequently experience small wins. Peters and Waterman speak of the importance of the leadership "publicly and ceaselessly lauding the small wins along the way."[8] When people are noticed, when they feel their colleagues care about them and want them to succeed, they gain meaning in their lives. They come to believe in the values of the company, and they want to share in their company's story.

It is the same for students. When students are noticed, when they are encouraged along the way, lauded publicly and ceaselessly, when they have many small wins to share with parents and relatives, with friends and peers, they are happier. When they feel that their teachers, principal, superintendent, school board, parents, and neighbors, all want them to win, they gain meaning in their lives, and they come to believe in the value of education and in the joy of learning. They also sharpen their own leadership skills. This is essential, for students must learn to be transforming leaders themselves. James MacGregor Burns says that "greatness in leadership is most likely to arise from 'creative local circumstances.'"[9] Schools and school districts can be those "creative local circumstances."

Transformational Leaders

Transformational leaders are those leaders who are in the process of being transformed. Their personality, their character, and their energy are being changed. They are becoming more positive than they already are, more open to listen, more willing to form partnerships, more prone to see the whole rather than a sliver or part.

Transformational leaders are more aware of the need to tap into their schools' rich culture, values, and story.

Who founded the school?

What were the conditions which brought it about?

What values were espoused by its early teachers and administrators?

What was it like to be one of the first students in the school?

What were these students' aspirations?

How were people educated in this town before there was a school?

Who were the people that made it happen?

How did the taxpayers feel about building a school?

Did some oppose the school, and if so, who were they and what was the point of their opposition?

When did the school begin "extra-curricular" activities?

How did kids learn these things before there were extra-curricular activities?

The stories and legends which make up the shared values and culture of schools and districts are some of the things which give identity to students, help them understand their roots, help them have responsibility to their school, and help make meaning in their lives.

Marva Collins knows well how engaging in the culture and shared values of school can offer an anchor to students. Principal at Westside Preparatory Academy, an inner-city school which she founded in Chicago, she taps into her own enriching story and from it gives hope to the students in her school. "My mother always told me I was a different child. I was always a reader and eager and curious about things. I always thought there was something besides the racism in Alabama. I've always been adventurous."[10] Her story ignites her teachers and together they ignite fire in their students: "My whole philosophy is to make the poor student as good as I can, and the good student superior," she says. "We have to do a lot of hugging and nurturing as well as teaching"; "The first step is for teachers to get to know their students and to love them"; "You just can't fake it with children, there's something innate in them, they know who cares."[11] Her story comes through in her words; there is a ring of truth in these quotes. Surely Marva Collins knows that getting people acting, even in small ways, will help them come to believe in what they are doing. She is a leader who understands transformation; understands what makes the sparks catch fire.

Some educators may say that they too would be more successful if they were in their own private schools, places where rules, regulations, and school boards did not shrink the vision and sap the spirit. This is only partially true. In the mid 1970s, the Council Bluffs, Iowa, school system had so many difficulties it was the subject of a *60 Minutes* television report. Mike Wallace pointed out that the school system was run down, the board of education was embroiled in internal strife, and that factionalism and polarization were rampant in the community.[12] Raj K. Chopra came as superintendent in 1978 and with his transformational leadership and ready followers, he quickly facilitated major change. He first changed the perception of the school system, then of the system itself. The Council Bluffs Schools continue to grow and build on this pride.

Transformational leaders find ways to make things happen even in the worst of circumstances. They view problems as challenges, they personally take responsibility for what they do; they get to know and become friends with their own bosses, and they establish trust levels that are very high. They usually find a way to resolve difficulty privately. Among professionals where superior-inferior relationships are the rule, where the trust level is minimal or does not exist at all, there are usually memoranda written in domineering language and phone conversations by the "boss" telling someone immediately to stop what they are doing or be "written up" for insubordination. No shared vision, no experiments, no tries, no creative action; only reaction and the erroneous belief that adherence to the rational method is all a leader needs.

In the dualistic approaches of the nineteenth and twentieth centuries, leaders in American education have separated out values, become rationalistic, and taught "whole-brained" students using mostly the "left-brained" methods of lecture and content-infusion. Hence, most schools are deficient in telling stories, in creating wonder, in sensing the need for expression of feelings and sharing values, in getting to know their students, and, in Marva Collins' words, in "loving them." But superintendents, principals, and teachers, who see themselves as transformational leaders wanting to change this situation, can begin by tapping into the history of their schools and showing how present staff and student uniqueness draws it out, strengthens it, and celebrates it. They can learn the art of storytelling themselves, and learn to engage students and parents in new and lively ways. Gradually, they will begin to repair the breach of dualism.

James MacGregor Burns offers a formula for transformational leadership. He says that it:

> . . . occurs when one or more persons *engage* with others in such a way that leaders and followers raise one another to higher levels of motivation and morality. Their purposes . . . become fused. Power bases are linked not as counterweights but as

mutual support for a common purpose . . . . Transforming leadership ultimately becomes *moral* in that it raises the level of human conduct and ethical aspiration of both the leader and the led, and thus has a transforming effect on both.[13]

Transformational leadership in education is a positive and validating force among colleagues. Educators have to engage each other, and to enter into enhancing interactions which raise one another to higher levels of motivation and morality. This is what Burns is talking about. Then they will be more excited about their jobs, more in touch with their own abilities to make a difference — better leaders and better teachers. Leaders who follow Burns' suggestions and for mutual support link their power bases have more trust in their colleagues and tend to trust the system. They are more committed because they feel more at home in their work environments, more sure of themselves and what they are doing, and more willing to share their power with others. This has enormous benefits in dealing with parents and the community for they lead from a power base which they do not have to question; they come from a colleague-support base which encourages. In *Making a Bad Situation Good,* Raj K. Chopra lists seven principles which could be called the principles of transformation needed by educational leaders:

Believe!

Look for the Good

Be Enthusiastic

Expect the Best

Determine to Make a Difference

Love and Laugh

Pursue the Dream[14]

Educational leadership that is transforming will live by these principles and use them in schools. They will help raise "the level of human conduct and ethical aspiration" of which Burns speaks, for they realize that the older world view is forever gone, and a new one, one which deals with the quality of life for the whole of creation, is being implemented. As Tom Hayden says:

In our fathers' time, democracy was threatened from abroad, our own institutions were basically sound, affluence appeared to most to be guaranteed, America was No. 1.

TRANSFORMING EDUCATION

> In our time we have received a different world view. Democracy has been threatened by "plumbers" operating from the White House, our institutions are troubled, affluence is hardly guaranteed, and being No. 1 in bombs hasn't made us No. 1 in the quality of life.[15]

Transformed educational leaders can help to implement new assumptions[16] which will undergird a transformed educational system so that all people can have quality in their lives. In addition to the seven principles put forth by Raj K. Chopra, leaders will be dealing with a new perspective. Rigid programs and schedules will need to be replaced by more flexible approaches to content and time. Change will come about by consensus through inspired leadership and inspired followership. Voluntarism will be high and there will be many mutual-help networks. Wherever feasible, there will be both a decentralizing of school systems and a sharing of power. Rather than power over others, which perpetuates "win/lose" situations and relationships, there will need to be power with others, which consistently offers "win/win" in situations and relationships. Schools and school systems will be characterized by respect for all people: students, teachers, helpers, volunteers. Pedagogy will include both the rational and the intuitive, and curricula will be both pragmatic *and* visionary. There will be emphasis on freedom and responsibility, on creativity, self-expression, self-knowledge, and on collective knowledge. "Transformation," "synergy," "empathy," and "transcendence" will be some of the terms used to characterize what transformed education is about. The human will be in partnership with nature, and sanity will refer not only to individuals, but to our interrelationships with the planet Earth. The new educational system will deal with the long-range, with ethics, with morality, with values, and with education's effect on the next seven generations. Experimentation will be encouraged, and programs will be designed to self-terminate.

Leaders who are themselves transformed will share these assumptions with the communities in which they lead. They will gladly offer their expertise to other leaders and other districts, knowing that there is increased power in sharing. They will also offer their expertise to, and make willing alliances with, businesses, social service agencies, churches, and synagogues in their districts. Transformed leaders realize that inclusion offers diversity, excitement, differentiation, and increased learning. Exclusion offers death.

School districts are fortunate because almost every one of them is in a neighborhood near best-run companies. Companies and schools could profit much by sharing their ideas and styles of leadership. School board members, superintendents, principals, and teachers, are only a phone call away from company management, which in many cases would welcome a professional relationship with educators. What is more, these professional relationships could blossom into friendships. In these relationships, new ideas in transforming leadership skills could become field-tested.

The resultant friendships, the genuine sharing, and the knowledge that others care about what educators are doing and that educators care about business, social service agencies, churches, and synagogues, will be a tremendous payoff not only personally, but for the schools, the companies, and the culture as well.

8

A New Paradigm for Learning

Sensing Needed Movement

As education realizes its important role in leadership, it will begin to lead in sensing needs in all areas. Transformational leaders sense needs early in the stream of life, before the need is so great upon the system that the only response is crisis management. Leadership that encourages openness among colleagues can be more responsive to needs, immediately when that is necessary, and can truly lead rather than play "catch up." There are many areas of education that need movement: curriculum, finance, teacher professionalism and salaries, teacher training, buildings, learning, empowerment of teachers, administrators, and students. The list could go on and on. Ten key areas of needed movement and ways for implementing change will be discussed here: building and buildings; co-teachers and shared learning; curriculum; textbooks; testing, grading and test scores; management; the role of the school board; property taxes and the taxation base; credentialing and student teaching; and educator in-service and staff development.

TRANSFORMING EDUCATION

Implementing Change in Ten Key Areas

Building and Buildings

The traditional approach to building and buildings keeps need, creativity, shared decision-making, citizen input (parents, students, and especially citizens who have no children), and business community input very low. Many professions operate like bureaucracies in that they think, design, and appropriate within a vacuum. Rather than go through the process of doing a self-study by asking the right questions, gathering information, and then having town hall meetings on educational concerns, administrators act in autocratic ways, quickly turning what is a needed and necessary process into a "them" and "us," "win-lose" situation. Decisions are made by the cognoscenti with little or no input from the citizens because education has been taken out of the realm of "leading out" and into the realm of control in which administrators know and ordinary citizens don't know.

What is necessary to counteract this mentality is a new understanding of place and space gleaned from the interconnections of the universe itself. A cosmic understanding of space allows for the realization that all of space is interconnected. Every part of the earth which we believe must be moved to build our schools needs to be looked at from the cosmic viewpoint.

> Will blasting a mountain or leveling a hill to make way for community needs really serve us best?
>
> Does it serve the planet best?
>
> What are the long range plans for this space?
>
> What will be needed fifty years from now?
>
> One hundred years from now?
>
> Are the proposed buildings the best use of the space?
>
> Do we need them?
>
> Do we want them?
>
> If we build them, will the space be enhanced because of their presence?

A NEW PARADIGM FOR LEARNING

What will the ecological balance be like after the building is built?

Must school take place inside a building?

Must the building be owned by the school district or can space be shared from among the many buildings under-utilized in any community, such as churches, movie theatres, community halls?

One of the marks of the universe is that it does not waste, nor does it produce waste. It renews, it recycles, it reverences, it is responsible, it uses the old to make the new. It adapts.

As more people offer input into education, and as people take control of their own lives and the life of their community, they will make decisions which are more harmonious with the environment and the needs of the community. If a building is needed, the community will have people within it that can design the space for it and then design the building. Children themselves can do preliminary sketches. Teachers can be asked their ideas and make sketches. People from other communities who have used this process can be invited to share their ideas, either in person or through videotape. Environmentalists, architects, city planners, builders, tradespeople, clergy, entrepreneurs, lawyers, gardeners, secretaries, students, taxpayers, cooks, stockbrokers, the employed and the unemployed—all need to share their ideas and the ideas of their unique perspective. This process may well take two or more years, but the members of the district will learn to know what they want, will get to know their neighbors, will learn how to barter and how to save and spend money, will collectively sense what education is about, will value more deeply themselves and their children. In this they will be practicing what the universe itself practices: holism and unification. Gone will be the power struggles of past and present; education will enter a new phase of power which empowers everyone.

In this cosmic understanding of place and space a new way of looking at the physical building will emerge. All the school buildings and other buildings used as schools need to be taken care of by those using them or by older students in the case of the very young. Students need to care for the entire building, from the grounds maintenance to the boilers and air conditioning, from the foundation to the roof, from the windows and shades to the intricacies of wiring and plumbing. Where city or county licenses are necessary, students and teachers can apply for them. Students and teachers can do it all. The work of running the building becomes itself part of any meaningful curriculum. School should not be viewed dualistically, where students pursue academics alone and the "maintenance department" looks after caring for buildings. The new curriculum will combine academics and responsibility for the buildings so that these parts of education will become mutually enhancing. Some educators may question if there will be enough time, especially with academic demands, but the question becomes moot when the educational system is understood in light of transformation. Students want to be needed, they want to learn new ways of caring for what they use, want to show pride in keeping up buildings which serve them so well. There is no need for janitorial staff, for cooks, for secretaries, for gardeners when within any school lies all the creative genius necessary to plan and execute any job necessary. Rather, the running of the building needs to be part of the daily routine of teachers and students. When students clean the bathrooms, they care for the bathrooms every time they use them. When students change the light bulbs they become more aware of when a light is needed and when it can be turned off. When students order paper and pencils, they become aware of needs and waste and their self-responsibility increases. Students caring for the lawns and growing some of the vegetables used in the cafeteria will learn about the cycles of the earth—planting, caring, growing, harvesting—and learn about their own selves and the inner core of their being. They will learn how to be and how to let go, they will learn a new definition of time, all things their ancestors knew well. "A time to plant, a time to sow, a time to reap," will help them measure their own growth with the progress of the seasons and the growth of the universe itself. Students repairing a roof will realize the importance of doing something correct the first time, as well as the importance of obtaining quality materials.

    Students need to care for the daily operations of the school also. They can answer the telephone, compose and write necessary letters, learn how and where to order supplies, learn how to barter their own and their fellow student's labor for extras for the school. They can schedule maintenance, make the repairs, and

A NEW PARADIGM FOR LEARNING

keep the files. They can wash the floors, wax the furniture, and wash the windows. They can paint the rooms, fix the furniture, and care for the school pets. Students can plan nutritious meals learned about because nutrition is part of their curriculum, cook the daily meals, serve, clean up, and help to compost and recycle the garbage. They can organize the cafeteria or organize other spaces which can better utilize space. They can plan and serve nutritious snacks for breaks.

Students who take part in the planning and maintaining and general upkeep of their building will not be vandals themselves, nor will they allow vandalism to take place either in school, in any public building or park in town, or on the streets. They will bring home valuable skills and help connect school with their home. Being verbs rather than nouns, they will be active and not passive in living, and they will live more fruitful and healthy lives. They will not be bored, nor plead ignorance when something breaks down. Instead, they will have a lively and active interest in *all* aspects of their education. They will begin early to learn of the great connectedness that exists in the universe and in themselves. They will learn the great value that is in work. Students who keep records and books, post ledgers, fill out tax forms, answer telephones, interview people, and work in administrators' offices, will learn valuable skills which will be used over their entire lifetime. They will sense their part in the universe, their unique gifts which they will willingly offer to others and to the planet. They will also have a better relationship with their parents as they talk with them and, on quarterly workdays, help initiate them into the life of the school buildings.

Co-teachers and Shared Learning

It is important that teachers teach. In traditional schools teachers spend a great deal of time doing other things: listening to complaints, dealing with disruptive behavior, filling out records, and expending negative energy because they feel cheated by their administration or because they are frozen in unrealistic expectations of students or because they feel like they get little or no support from colleagues, parents, and the community. Teachers who are freed to teach, to provoke, to enable, to create, to promote, to empower, to play, have high and positive energy, and they teach.

TRANSFORMING EDUCATION

In the last quarter century, movement throughout the world has been toward sharing: shared leadership, shared work, shared living, shared parenting, and shared creating. Education, too, can be more powerful if teaching is shared. Co-teachers enable each other and students, free each other to do in the classroom what each does best, and allow each to have a deeper relationship with students.

It might be asked where the extra money will come from in these times of state and federal bills limiting expenditures for all agencies. What is proposed will cost virtually nothing extra because American society is fortunate to have a large group of skilled teachers who will flock to the classrooms across the country and work almost for free if they are only asked. This group of skilled teachers is the large senior adult community living in high-rise or low-rise housing or in their own homes in every state and in almost every community. People who have made their mark in life, who have achieved, who have found the ways to expand their insights, their years, and their living. These people would not only welcome the opportunity to serve as co-teachers in the classrooms of America's schools; they would *celebrate* it. They have the energy, they have the desire, and most especially, they have the time and the lived experiences to enable and encourage. Many senior adults feel unneeded and unwanted. As co-teachers in the classroom, they will feel needed, wanted, and their own esteem will be enhanced. Any of us shines when asked our opinion, asked how we coped with a boyfriend or girlfriend, with our parents, asked what it was like for us when we were the age of the children we teach. Senior adults can teach and oversee the repairs of the buildings, can listen, can hug, can support, can add the dimensions missing in present child rearing approaches. They can assist teachers in teaching lessons and in many other tasks. They have a bevy of friends whom they can approach for a tailor-made presentation on any subject. They have an unabashed ability to ask for what they need and their presence will communicate honesty and straightforwardness. They would rather work for the intrinsic rewards of knowing they are making a contribution to humankind than for a salary for doing what they were told to do. They know good stories, and many are excellent storytellers.

Children of all ages, especially teenagers, get along with senior adults tremendously well. Neither group has a lot of fear: teenagers because they have not yet learned fear, and senior adults because they have worked through their fears and have let them go. Both groups are open to exploration, to questioning, to taking risks. Shared teaching produces a mutuality of "brain-picking," wondering, playing, and validating among all the members of the class. In this atmosphere regular teachers will become enriched rather than burned out and will have an immediate colleague to share the burdens with rather than being the only responsible adult.

Making co-teaching happen is not difficult at all. However, educators have really to want it for it to be effective. If regular teachers feel threatened, do not want to share their authority, feel jealous, or feel they "may be found out" (that is, they hold a belief that they are supposed to know everything and now another adult knows what students knew all along—that they do not), then co-teaching is not going to work. Effective teaching for the new age demands co-teaching. There may be more than two co-teachers. There may be many who come from time to time or on different days of the week to be with the regular teacher. Among willing adults, more can be done over a potluck planning session than will ever be done by one frustrated teacher trying to do it all. The co-teaching model becomes a great modeling experience for students to learn. Many students' homes are fragmented. Many students feel alienated, frustrated, angry, and alone. Being in a co-teaching environment puts them in touch with relationships which work, which enhance, which grow; ultimately relationships in which they themselves will want to share. They will come to realize that both teaching and learning is shared, that we build on the shoulders and track records of others, and that we are all interrelated and interconnected. Learning experiences can replace the pressure to learn and peer pressure will give way to peer encouragement because several adults will be available to students as anchors in their lives. Also, because of the relationships formed with these senior adults, latchkey problems presently experienced in America, will be lessened. Students whose parents are working could go home with the senior adults, meet their friends in the high-rise, make new adult friends, and have higher quality in their lives than they do going home to an empty house or going to a shopping mall.

Senior adults who have classroom experiences will contribute much to citizen dialogues and taxpayer meetings. They will tell supportive stories about teachers and administrators, and offer supportive input to school boards and other governing bodies. They will feel useful in the democratic process. They will also have relationships with the parents of their students and in effect become co-parents. As parents feel that their children's teachers and co-teachers care, they will be more willing to take an active part in the education of their children. Co-teaching is a model which exemplifies and enhances as it amplifies and encourages. It is a model—much like the universe itself—where not only all creation works together for mutual enhancement, but where all are winners and keep on winning.

Curriculum

Much has already been said about curriculum in chapter 6. Suffice it to say here that to transform the educational curriculum, needs will have to be sensed and addressed early. This means that a part of education will need to be open to change and staying in the forefront of thinking and experience. Yet a part of education will need to be a foundation, an anchor, not resistant to change but aware that some change is a fad and may not be beneficial. In other words, education has to be truly dialectic, with dynamic energy coming from the myriad activities created by its tension. Practically, it means offering instruction in computers while not sacrificing basic math, spelling, and typing skills. It means gardening, and reading literature, playing games and taking camping trips, and working "thinkers" in the classroom, caring for the buildings and grounds, and caring for the body through good nutrition. It means caring for others through hospitality programs and cultural exchanges. It means instilling compassion and actively working for peace. Educators need to be open to the new, get excited by the different, and be willing to put forth the unconventional to all students, while at the same time maintaining integrity with the goals of the educational process: students being led from where they are, encouraged to take risks, while being grounded in fundamental skills, and enhancing their sense of responsibility through new ideas and through accepting the consequences of their actions.

Textbooks

While textbooks are looked upon as setting parameters for the educational process, that is, naming the content of what it is that a class will study, they have become a burden on several fronts. First, they are a burden because many teachers view the textbook as a bible, in which everything a student is "supposed" to learn and know is contained. When a student has "learned" this material and sufficiently gives it back on tests, he or she is said to "have" it; that is, mastered it. This is very confining and is a poor view of the learning process.

Secondly, textbooks in some fields become outdated quickly and many times are so general that they give only a surface explanation of a situation without inviting the reader into more depth.

The third way in which textbooks are a burden is that they represent an enormous unnecessary expense to schools and school districts. Books already in libraries, tapes, videos, and stories from others, and all interactions which are humane and human, promote learning. Important ideas found in textbooks could be placed on newsprint or photocopied. Children can make their own textbooks out of what they draw, write, and collect. Some may want to challenge this as naive, but a book made by a student becomes a treasure to be savored and the relearning process is deeper when we live through our treasures. With textbooks, we are not allowed to mark them, to draw in them, to use a "hi-liter" to connect ideas in one chapter with a similar idea in another. We are not allowed to have them after the year in which we used them; and few of us have ever wanted to save a textbook anyway. Textbooks are impersonal, cold, and clinical. Books that are handmade by individuals have a warmth about them and retain this warmth throughout the years. Memory is important for our growth and development, and the memory contained in our own handmade textbooks will be significant in our lives always.

In "The Search for Excellence In Science Education," John E. Penick and Robert E. Yager comment on the decreased value of textbooks. They mention that teachers who are given time to develop science curricula and extensive in-service to help develop their ideas have exemplary programs in their schools. They say, "The curricula that result from these efforts are almost entirely locally developed . . . . Textbooks are usually not very visible;

where they are visible, they usually play a secondary role, as resources and references."[1]

It must be remembered that printing and the printed word came relatively late in our evolution. Up to the fifteenth century, story, oral tradition, and art and art forms were the way of handing on information. Common to these forms was human interaction, thinking, and feedback. Reliance on textbooks and the printed word may be important, but they can never replace human interaction and personal art forms developed by students.

Testing, Grading, and Test Scores

Testing sends a negative message to students, helps put them in turmoil before, during, and after the test, and puts teachers and those administering tests in a authoritarian environment which causes students to pay lip service rather than to develop self-responsibility. Clearly, there are better ways of bringing out the best in each of us. All motivation is self-motivation, and without students seeing a need to do something, to study further, they will have little motivation to do so. Some educators hold for a reward system; although this has its positive aspects, education should enable students to be able to achieve what they want because they desire it and because they receive intrinsic rewards, whether it has external rewards or not. Educators need to create environments in which students will value their own achievements, *no matter what these may be.* In *Wad-Ja-Get?,* subtitled "The Grading Game in American Education," Howard Kirschenbaum, Sidney B. Simon, and Rodney W. Napier tell of students who decided to write an article on grading in their high school newspaper. What they had written is important and worth probing. It dealt with a poetry assignment in English class and whether or not it should be graded. Here is some of what they said:

> . . . let's face it. Everyone wants good grades and will do whatever he can to get them. If the school does not give grades for creativity, then students will not make any effort to be creative. They will spend their time and energy doing those things which *will* be rewarded.[2]

The students succinctly set the grading dilemma in its rightful context. When grades become the most important part of education, then education and the learning process itself takes a back

A NEW PARADIGM FOR LEARNING

seat, and *any* method of getting a "good" grade becomes primary. Stanford University recently endured a cheating scandal because of the importance placed on grades. A graduate student wrote in the *Stanford Daily* that the honor code should be trashed. "It (the code) certainly benefits cheaters," she said.[3] It was reported that the scandal erupted because psychology professor Philip Zimbardo changed a psychology course which had a longtime reputation as an easy "A" with little work to one giving students a lot of reading and difficult tests.

The high school students quoted in *Wad-Ja-Get?* said: "Finally, we're against grading because it encourages cheating. From what we've seen, most people in this school cheat, in one way or another."[4] Once the push is on for grades bizarre behavior arises in students. It is one way they deal with the fight or flight mechanism in each of us which rears its head every time a stressor is presented.

Testing, grading, and test scores are questionable, but if they are to be helpful, they need to be self-applied, that is, placed on students by the students themselves. Testing needs to be seen in light of a *celebration of knowledge,* for that is what is behind asking students to share their insights. When knowledge is celebrated, students, teachers, administrators, parents, and people from the community all share in the event. This has to be done in a pressure-free atmosphere, an environment that is warm, caring, and open. The celebration of knowledge would encompass all aspects of education and would come through varied mediums. One part of it could be answering questions, even writing the answers down, and later sharing them with small groups or with a larger group. Asking questions, receiving feedback, clarifying a student's thinking—these are the goals of the celebration. As part of the process, students could grade themselves, and that grade could become part of their record. Often adults are uncomfortable with students' self-grading because they believe that students will unfairly give themselves higher grades. This is usually not the case, but if it were, what would be wrong about that? Students would soon come face to face with the knowledge that they are cheating themselves, and in a positive atmosphere would see the need to change their practices. When students grade themselves they consistently grade *under* where a teacher would grade them. Celebrations of knowledge and self-grading build self-confidence

159

and increase self-esteem. They open students to all types of learning, rather than that which can be graded easily, such as true-false and multiple choice tests. They make students responsible for their learning rather than turning them into robots. Also, celebrations of knowledge and self-grading moves teachers out of the authoritarian syndrome and into empowerment. Studs Terkel makes this point in *Working*:

> You get into a classroom and you have all the power of the institution. You tell people what to do and they do it, what to read and they read it. You tell people what to think, how to interpret things . . . . You can make them feel guilty because they haven't read certain things, because they're not familiar with them.[5]

The students that Kirschenbaum, Simon, and Napier spoke about say ". . . we're scared of many of our teachers because of the power that grading gives them over us."[6] They also said they do not feel that grades are fair. They cite a comparison of one student who has trouble in French, who works hard, and gets a "C," to another student who finds French easy, does not work at it, and gets a "B." "Is that fair?,"[7] they rightfully ask. They go on to offer educators great wisdom: "If a student really tries hard in a subject and gets a low grade, he might get discouraged and stop trying."[8] That is precisely what happens to large numbers of students every day in school. They get discouraged and stop trying. The students quoted above finish their article saying: "We think this would be a much better school if marks were completely eliminated."[9]

In Waldorf Schools there are no marks in the elementary grades and marks only begin in high school so that students can compete with other high school students for college placement, because grades and tests scores are *the* barometer of entrance into these institutions.

American education is in a unique place to exercise leadership for our own schools and be a model for other educational systems. One way it can achieve this is to drop grading and testing and turn instead to celebrations of knowledge and self-grading. This could be easily done from the elementary to university level. This means that other criteria will need to be found and spelled out for college entrance. For the high school and college student perhaps it would be simply the criteria that a student wishes to be there, wishes to work in a certain curriculum area, and wishes to celebrate his or her knowledge in a meaningful way. Tea[chers and] professors could hold an open house in which they share [their] expertise, their specialty, and their style. Students could [make a] selection based on their intuition and their own investigati[on.] They could then inquire about signing on as apprentices to these teachers and professors. In this system, educators will be getting back to the true notion of a school, a place of leisure, a center of diversity.

Management

In speaking about what a good educational system should have, Ivan Illich lists three purposes:

> It should provide all who want to learn with access to available resources at any time in their lives; empower all who want to share what they know to find those who want to learn it from them; and finally, furnish all who want to present an issue to the public with the opportunity to make their challenge known.[10]

As in any system, form should follow function and not the other way around. What is the function of management in any corporation or institution? It is to create the methods whereby the goals and purposes of the institution will be carried out in the most effective and ethical way possible, and to ensure the funding and communication necessary so that the methods can be ongoing.

In educational systems, management needs to be looked at very carefully. It is frequently top-heavy, one-sided, sexist, and entrenched. All too often the "Peter Principle" is alive and well among the educational hierarchy. Administrators who have not had to be accountable in many years become stuck in positions of power in which teachers are forced to defer to their length of years in that position. Schools need to employ management which is open so that Illich's three purposes can be adopted. In a compulsory educational system all who want to learn need to be provided the means of that learning. It becomes dualistic to make education compulsory and then not provide the means by which to attain what we force people to acquire.

Illich's first point has a wider application than just providing the typical public school services. Creative leadership, together with parents, students, and taxpayers can well expand schooling concepts to take in home schooling, a meaningful voucher system, alternative schools, private and parochial schools, and a type of "university of the streets," common in many inner cities. Management that is available to listen, open to change, responsive to needs of citizens now, can find creative ways to make this wider education work. This can be done without necessarily constructing more buildings. What is called for is meaningful dialogue in which all who want to can have input. From this dialogue can come a plan or plans which the community can talk about, deal with, interact over, and generally come to agreement on. It may be that one school will hold art classes at a downtown studio once a week, with students getting there on their own, either walking, using public transportation, or parental carpools. What management needs to do and do well is to provide access to the available resources for all who want them. To do this, traditional educational approaches and designs will have to change from being secretive ideas and places with secretive plans where educators alone unlock knowledge, to places where information, ideas, and desires are freely put on the educational table for any and all to pick up and use.

Illich's second purpose of a good educational system focuses on shared knowledge. If a student wants to learn Vietnamese and finds someone in the neighborhood who can teach him or her, then management needs to facilitate that happening without getting caught up in outdated models of credentialing or other roadblocks. If the student surpasses the teacher, then the student will of his or her own motivation move on to someone who can give more. If a student wants to learn to cook and a restaurant cook wants to take on this teaching, then educational management needs to have a process in which this can be quickly facilitated. What is being proposed here is not an unfocused education that is helter skelter but the freedom to see education in a wider sense, with many of society's activities as classrooms of the here and now, presided over by responsive management capable of acting quickly, recognizing the ability of varied teachers, and validating and encouraging students of all ages.

Illich's third purpose "to furnish all who want to present an issue to the public with the opportunity to make their challenge known," is important and can empower whole communities. One of the ways that personal power is gained is through choices, and the choice of taking a risk and speaking out in public offers great growth in personal power. When people can say what they want to say and be accepted or not on their own merits, personal power takes a great leap forward. In today's complex and bureaucratic society many citizens feel unempowered and alienated. Many youth feel they have no voice. Using the schools as places of public forum for anyone who wants to share their message, offers people and the community a chance to come to grips with various situations. Almost every town and city has those who write letters to the editor in their newspaper, sometimes a few who do it frequently. Oftentimes they are citizens blowing off steam, but sometimes the steam makes enormous sense. What would happen to these people if they were denied a forum? Perhaps their blowing off steam would issue forth in violence. Using the schools as places of public forums makes the schools living and breathing entities in communities. Visitors to Faneuil Hall in Boston are proudly told the history of the Hall which was donated to the City by Peter Faneuil in 1742. James Otis dubbed the Hall the "Cradle of Liberty" because of the protests of British policy voiced there. During the Vietnamese War citizens held public meetings and debates. The Hall can still be rented by anybody for town and public meetings. Schools need to become "Cradles of Liberty" freely available to any and all citizens of the community who pay for the support of the buildings. To do this, management will have to learn to trust the wisdom of the citizens. This may be difficult at first because of administrator beliefs that "we have the answers." Schools should be available for any and all purposes that fit democracy, and they should be seen as extensions of citizens' homes, freely available places of great coming together and learning.

Another role of management is to support teachers to the maximum. Management has the ability to be constant validators of teachers and principals. Superintendents need to be informed, intelligent, and creative validators who *personally* know each teacher and principal and who come to know generally *every* student. If they cannot do this, it is a major tip-off that the district is too big, or that management is too caught up in the business of running things rather than being available for teachers, children, and parents. A big job? Yes, but also quite workable by responsible managers. What a great day it will be for teachers when they can call their superintendent to say that they need a mental health day, that they have arranged for a colleague and other co-teachers to stand in for them, and the superintendent will *congratulate* them for wanting to *renew* themselves so that they have *more* to offer their students and the district!

A further word on management must be said. When teachers are assisted by co-teachers, when parents are intimately brought into the schools, when decisions about schooling are shared, when all citizens have input into schools, then teachers and co-teachers will be freed to teach and make decisions that will benefit the education of all. There will be no need for middle management consultants in school districts. When teachers receive colleague support, when they are believed in and validated by their principals and superintendents, they will be encouraged to do what they do best — teach. Of course, they will need staff development and in-service, but they will not need coordinators, specialists, or consultants to teach them and their students about self-esteem. Obviously these coordinators and life-skills specialists are capable in their fields, but they will not be needed because teachers will develop the abilities they need in these areas themselves, especially in self-esteem, or they will bring people with these skills into the classroom. Many schools feel they cannot bring outsiders into the classroom because their budgets are already strained. There are many ways of "paying" a guest lecturer-teacher: some will come for free, others can be paid from a guest lecturer's fund established by all schools, some by having the children make something to offer to the guest, some by bartering. Citizens in all walks of life, both those in corporate structures and entrepreneurs in private practices, welcome the opportunity to go into the schools and share their skills and their messages. Students respond enthusiastically to these people because they have an opportunity to get to know them and in some cases develop personal or mentor relationships with them. This can do wonders for students who want to follow a dream or test the waters of a perceived career.

The Role of the School Board

People who serve on school boards have a wonderful opportunity to lead their communities. Their main role is to help the community develop policies that will expand the minds of students and

A NEW PARADIGM FOR LEARNING

all citizens. Members of the board have to be knowledgeable or willing to learn in several areas: management, finance, taxation, curriculum, art, architecture, an understanding and respect of how the universe works and their own place in the evolutionary process, values and the valuing process, group leadership and interaction, and vision.

Frequently citizens run for a seat on the school board because something in the community is perceived as a "crisis" and they have a strong opinion pro or con on it. This explains why some school boards suffer such polarization. What is needed is a type of disciplining, that is, people who serve the schools in various ways, for example, as co-teachers, teacher aides, helpers of students in such programs as PEER, driver education, sex education, curriculum development, coaching, etc. People who have had a chance to give some of their expertise to the school or district and who share the common educational vision could then be selected or elected by their communities to serve on the board. Serving as a school board member is far more than a popularity contest, also far more than a single issue focus. Board members need to get to know their constituents and meet frequently with them for input and decision-making.

One role of the board has been to hire and fire superintendents. Over the last two decades it has become routine for many boards to hire a consulting firm to make a "national search" for this important post. Three things happen when this takes place: first, a valuable learning experience which will help the board and the community is lost forever because it is handed over to some outside consulting firm which has its commission as its bottom line. The consulting firm has no fixed interest in the community for which it recruits. There may be some follow-up from the better consulting firms, but essentially this is a single action process quite removed from the citizens of a district.

Secondly, school boards dilute their personal and corporate power when they hire consulting firms. They in essence say that "this job is too much for us to handle," or "we do not know enough about the process," or "we are not intelligent enough to make the right choice." In this they miss what education really is. Education takes one from the unknown into the known or at least into that which becomes more familiar and comfortable. Selecting a superintendent is a great learning process, one in which every school board member develops a sharpened ability to think, to intuit, to create, to enable, to interact with citizens, to decide, and ultimately, to live with the consequences of their decision. The selection process should be a microcosm of the macrocosm going on in classrooms all across the nation. This is the height of education—learning. It is part of our cultural dualism that a typical district pays between fifteen and fifty thousand taxpayer dollars for a superintendent search and in the process loses far more than it gains.

Finally, the present selection process serves to model fragmentation to an already fragmented and alienated group of people: administrators, teachers, students, parents, and taxpayers. Education that is holistic serves to bring people together, not to push them apart. Education that is holistic wants issues placed clearly and cleanly on the table for all to see and discuss. People who are part of the decision-making process usually live more easily with what they have collectively wrought than had they had no meaningful input. Some might say that in the present process there is input. That is true, but the input is so meagre, and the process so obfuscating, that many citizens feel they have no power, and students and parents feel that the issues are already decided. Indeed, many times they are!

Another role of school board members is to look at both the present and the future and frequently ask themselves, "How can we help to better the educational experience?" Many districts need to deal with ideas which have passed their prime: busing, using schools for only nine months, decreeing daily operations from 8 A.M. to 4 P.M., restricting use of swimming pools and school property. Board members need to look into a more cooperative mode, one which allows citizens to use school grounds for garden plots, one which allows the buildings to be used 24 hours a day if that makes sense to a community, one that supports most children walking to school for their own health and exercise, one that gets citizens to share their private libraries, art, and other collections, one that offers citizens a chance to come into schools to share their expertise in cooking, sewing, painting, and other creative tasks.

School board members also need to look to the future, to research needs, to offer contracts to teachers, and to judge teachers brought before the board for alleged infractions of their contracts. Here too, there is a valuable learning process for all involved. Although privacy needs to be respected for all parties, teacher infractions and contract negotiations can be educational helps for the community if they are handled openly.

In the case of contract renewals discussion needs to begin long before contracts come up for renewal. As more parents, taxpayers, and students have input into the process, the whole community can sense the worth of their teachers and begin thinking more openly and compassionately toward them, become more validating of them. With students caring for buildings, with decreased vandalism costs to buildings, with businesses, churches, and synagogues offering rooms and buildings on a part-time basis for schools' use, with no consultant and coordinator salaries to pay, with superintendents and other managers receiving salaries that are more on a par with teachers in the classrooms—perhaps equal with teachers with the same seniority, districts will have money available to raise teacher salaries to be competitive with other professions, and to make available increased amounts of money for events and material, to make scholarship and debt retirement funds available, as well as making investments for future needs.

Property Taxes and the Taxation Base

Few words are as laden with emotionalism as taxation. Just about everybody has some thoughts and feelings about it, and many regard taxation as something very negative. Part of the legend surrounding the "founders" of the nation says that they wanted to escape "unjust" taxation. Taxation has been with us since ancient times and rather than being a negative concept it needs to be seen positively. This may be difficult because of its emotional charge. It consumes a lot of our thinking and time. We are reminded of it almost weekly as it takes a bite out of our paychecks. It is reported daily in newspapers across the country. Politicians like to manipulate tax bases by purporting to lower taxes while increasing goods and services or calling for higher taxes that will only minimally affect taxpayer income while the new taxation supplies everything from new roads and bridges to apple pie. In addition, businesses and individuals play the tax avoidance game, usually trying to find loopholes to avoid as much tax as they can.

In essence, taxation collectively pays for those things a society could not have because individuals alone would not have the ability to supply them; for example, libraries, parks, art galleries, historic structures, health systems, roads, a legal and court system, traffic systems, police and fire protection, protection of the country, salaries for political people and processes, and schools. Taxes need to be levied, collected, invested, and spent to ensure delivery of certain goods and services. Historically, schools were funded by property taxes with wealthy communities providing a larger tax base—and seemingly "better" schools—than poorer communities. Schools are still funded by property tax, but other taxes are levied by the state and administered as part of the state's school budget. In depressed areas the federal government pays a share. In some states it is becoming fashionable for lotteries to fund part of their educational needs. State departments of public instruction, with legislative approval, usually administer the payment of tax monies in a fixed per diem, per capita amount to districts. When a student moves or is absent, the district loses the per capita money.

As more citizens have a voice in education, as students feel better about their schooling and validate themselves and their schools, as business, schools, individuals, school boards, and educators cooperate with each other for the common shared vision, peoples' view of taxes and taxation will change. Rather than being perceived as a "necessary evil," taxation can be perceived as a meaningful commitment. People will then want to fund schools and will want to pay taxes, at least the taxes that fund smiles on the faces of students and educators. This is not a naive view. People gladly pay for what they *believe in.* As the citizens of a school district come to believe in that district's educational values, they will willingly fund them. But it cannot happen if the school system is sick, or if educators, students, and parents bad-mouth the schools, the educational system, and the educational process. Nor can it happen if people do not have a voice in their educational system. As taxpayers come to know the schools in an intimate way, as they are invited to offer ideas and feedback, as they see their ideas put into practice, as they come to have a personal relationship with teachers and students, they will desire to help fund educational endeavors. There are many people of only modest means who continually fund scholarships for students because they want them to have the opportunity to have new doors opened to them, to learn new skills.

Finally there needs to be a celebratory aspect to taxation. This can be done quite well by schools as was shown earlier in describing situations where students and teachers would have programs in neighborhoods. As part of Raj K. Chopra's leadership, the Council Bluffs, Iowa school district began an annual "Pride Parade" which successfully highlighted the schools' contribution to the life of the city.[11] When taxpayers see what their tax dollars are accomplishing, they may be quite willing to even consider the idea of increasing their property taxes to fund new ideas and a better future for our children and the generations to come.

Credentialing and Student Teaching

In the specialization that has taken place since the end of the Second World War, credentialing has almost taken on a life of its own, becoming so symbolic that it is the golden ring on the carousel ride towards teaching. Credentials are important and necessary so that citizens are assured that teachers have a certain expertise in their professions. However, the process itself needs to be overhauled in at least two areas: first, the human values needed to be a responsible teacher. These human values—which must be in the fabric of every teacher and need to be an integral part of the credentialing process—are the ability to listen, to encourage, to admire, to trust, and to be open to children, parents, and community.

Secondly, the process as it is, is too sterile and too narrowly defined. It takes place principally in schools of education at the university level rather than at the classroom and district level where citizens could have input. There is some classroom participation, usually for one semester of "practice teaching," but nothing longer, no attempt to live with a family of students and really get to know students' minds, hearts, and desires. The latter is especially needed by new teachers who are younger and have not yet begun their families. The argument may be made that attorneys get credentialed without citizen input or without living with another attorney's family. They at least have their fellow attorneys who work in the same field making recommendations, and they have standardized criteria. College and university schools of education usually do not. Some schools of education have mandatory human values courses which aspiring teachers must do well in, but there are no national criteria, and the variance among the states is indeed high. The initial credentialing process which includes practice teaching does not have all the teachers in a building even getting to know the student teacher. The student teacher is adrift in a field, usually with most of the input coming only from the teacher with whom he or she is practicing. That teacher makes recommendations to the principal, and after a semester of proper lesson plans and a developed ability to put information *into* students, and after "successfully" completing the required college courses, the candidate becomes a newly ordained teacher. After that there is a process, usually within each five years of teaching, of taking a minimum number of college credits to maintain the credential.

One place where the tide can begin to turn is in student teaching. Presently what most practice teaching amounts to is watching the regular teacher and helping out with minor chores. John Holt says: "To expect anyone to learn to teach by such methods is like expecting a child to learn to drive a car by sitting in his parents' laps and holding the wheel while they steer it."[12] Because student teachers need good reports in a system that has little fixed criteria, they are reluctant to risk new or novel ideas that their cooperating teachers may not like or approve. Hence, the creativity these people could bring to the classrooms, the breath of fresh air they could bring to the teachers, is all but missing.

Student practice teaching could be made much more dynamic. First, student teachers need more than a brief look inside a classroom. Field experience is precisely that, "experience" in the field. It refers to more than a brief encounter in one or two classrooms for one semester. John Holt comments that:

> A more helpful way to train people for the work of teaching in classrooms would be to have them *begin* by teaching real classes in real schools, all the while giving them places and plenty of time to talk about their work with other new teachers in the same position, sometimes (but not always) in the company of a sympathetic and more experienced teacher.[13]

During these discussions, backed by insights gleaned from the rereading of teaching and psychology books, they can make sense of their beginning teaching experience. Here too, is where the questions of Sid Simon used earlier can make a big difference. "What did *you* learn?" "What would you do differently if you could do it again?" And the greatest question any teacher, administrator, or superintendent can ask all people, especially aspiring teachers, "What do you need from me?" Out of these active experiences, discussions, readings, and reflections, these newly recognized teachers could perhaps write their own manuals, their own guides. These could be a boon for the newly beginning teacher because they would have been written by someone actually going through the experience rather than by professors who are writing about their own experience of twenty years ago.

Those who would be teachers or helpers of any kind who have never raised a child need the experience of a warm and loving family with small children to hone their teaching abilities. Infants and small children are masters at learning and *they teach* adults how it is that children learn. They will, in a very short time, teach any educator what is wrong with present classroom learning and what is right about how learning takes place. In the last year of college future teachers who have not been parents could live with a family, care for the children and *learn* from them and the family's interactions. After the first semester of living with the family, questioning, learning from that family, seeing group interactions, understanding how some problems fade away, or do or do not get solved, and how pain is dealt with, they could teach a class at the local school. The family with whom they lived would be available daily for discussions, for sharing of insights, for shared learning. They could also meet each Sunday evening at a potluck with other teachers and their administrators for mutual encouragement. Superintendents especially should want to be with these new teachers for it is their chance to see future bright lights on the educational horizon. Under the superintendent's tutelage, new teachers can feel the warmth of a caring environment and watch their own growth blossom. This invaluable experience would be a learning laboratory for these new teachers. Their training would be hands-on, their ideas would be child-based, their joys and sorrows would be real, their creativity bubbling.

Student teachers living with families could help families feel more fulfilled also. Families would have co-parents for a school year, and student teachers would have the help of "co-teachers" from all the family members helping them hone their insights and learn from their experiences. Schools of education would benefit from taking this creative approach and would put less importance on papers and reports required before the experience—which at best are passive.

Families would need to be paid not just for housing and meals but for their part in the student's education. For the first time students would actually feel that they were getting their money's worth from paying student teaching costs. In dealing with these families, colleges also would create a number of new contacts for their own classes and future enrollment. Finally, colleges would have a chance to separate the wheat from the chaff in their own education departments. As John Holt says: "Any education professors who need piles of paper to prove that their students are learning anything would be better off left out of such a program."[14] After this experience of living in a family for a school year and teaching one's own class for a semester, the student could spend the summer writing their experiences. Now they will be writing from first-hand experiences, and their papers will make enormous sense. Furthermore, they will be well on their way towards developing a vehicle for sharing these experiences with others, and that is where more learning takes place. Based on reports that parents, students (if they are mature enough), and the host family members make, combined with professional educators and the degree granting schools, and their own input, future teachers could be credentialed.

Monitoring the student teacher's progress needs to be an open and ongoing process. This means that college schools of education need to have a high level of intimacy between students and faculty. Student evaluation should also be an ongoing process. At the end of quarters or semesters, instructors, with the student, should complete an evaluation form indicating the credit status, and describing the student's academic performance and personal growth and leadership progress in the class. Credit should be given upon completion of learning contracts made by the student. A general review of student progress should take place each fall and spring. Students found to be deficient in academic or personal growth and leadership progress should be encouraged to deal with the deficiency.

All aspects of the college's education school should count equally. Both cognitive and affective approaches to learning need to share the same importance. As feedback is a constant process, the monitoring of a student's progress should be constantly and consistently known to the student, the faculty, and administration. Thus the college does not get caught in the bind of surprises, either on the part of the student, or faculty and administration. As coursework is sequentially ordered, students progress intelligently, always building on previous experience. By the time of student teaching the student will have a definite idea of how and where to proceed. With constant faculty, administration, and colleague encouragement, and the encouragement of the family with whom the student lives, there is a positive atmosphere set up, one in which the student is bound to succeed.

Every five years teachers should go through a thorough process of review for the maintenance of their credential. This review process should include dialogue with administrators, colleagues, parents, and taxpayers. Through the five years teachers should participate in workshops, college courses, travel, and in-services, and there should be semester or quarter reports offering feedback from colleagues and administrators, and where appropriate, reports from students themselves. Some teachers may want to argue these points, but a meaningful feedback process can assure greater fairness both in the teacher's professional life and in their personnel folder while at the same time helping teachers become better at their craft, opening them to new ideas in their classrooms. The *process* is important and ought not to have "grades" attached to it. Its function is for meaningful feedback, information, and dialogue. If a teacher is not up to professional standards, that will be pointed out through the process; then administrators can offer to help the teacher meet the criteria, get needed help or counseling, change some situations in the classroom, get more colleague and administration support, take a rest, or, if necessary, help the teacher transfer to another profession.

Educator In-service and Staff Development

This is an area of great variance among school districts and states. Some have excellent in-service; many do not. Universally there is a great drawback in educator and teacher in-service. Frequently, it is seen more as a panacea than as a part of ongoing staff development; often it is unplanned, uncoordinated with the future, and there is little understanding as to how the in-service holistically aids education. In some cases superintendents and principals hire in-service providers because of an existent problem which they hope the provider will address and solve.

Good in-service should provide excellent staff development. Education is not only for students but must be a planned and ongoing part of development of the staff also. Educators, teachers, and support personnel must remember they are students, too. The more ideas they share, the more they realize their own and others' roles, the more training they can receive in self-esteem and personal self-confidence, the more they can overcome communication barriers and manipulation and make guilt-free decisions — the more efficiently a classroom or office runs and the more creativity and productivity can be realized. Training teachers and educators to learn and practice management skills, to understand better how and where support comes from, to befriend the earth, and to realize consistently each individual's contribution to the overall effort, is an important part of developing staff. As educators and teachers develop their professional lives, the quality of their personal, social, family life, and the life of the planet also increases. They become people who have more to offer, who seldom suffer burnout, who can create strategies for using time intelligently and economically; people who can recognize their own strengths and weaknesses, and feel comfortable sharing their lives professionally.

In the classroom, teachers who have been exposed to excellent staff development engage in the process of unlearning as much as they engage in the process of new learning: unlearning some long-standing teacher beliefs that cause grief and stress, that keep them from change, that keep them from building on a new foundation. They help students develop realistic student beliefs because they themselves are constantly reassessing their own teacher beliefs. They help students redirect negative goals and emotion for positive goals and emotion. They engender cooperation because they view themselves as co-winners with everyone else. They know the difference between "you" and "I" messages, and they are more willing to disclose themselves. They also are willing to view their class as a group, aware of group dynamics and the power a group of turned-on students have for their own betterment and the betterment of their schools and community. Finally, teachers who have had and continue to participate in meaningful in-service, are more prone to view their students as the "precious resources," the "national treasures," they really are.

Staff development and in-service work best when teachers and administrators take a day off away from school. A retreat center, a country club, a cabin in a park, a museum, a time of midweek camping, or time at a bed and breakfast; these make good places for a day of in-service. Meals could be provided or cooperatively planned and prepared. Preconceived negative attitudes and rank of any kind usually pale when superintendents and principals work side by side with teachers and co-teachers peeling potatoes or making their favorite curry sauce for the chicken. These days of in-service should be held monthly except when they stretch to two or more days at some point in each quarter. Outside consultants, some of whom could be former teachers who have become entrepreneurs knowledgeable in diverse areas, can be brought in for these times of staff development. Some of the presenters could be teachers and administrators from other districts too. Teachers should be able to have input into the planning and content of the in-service days as well as able to pick the in-service area in which they would like to participate. If a science teacher is suffering extreme grief because of the death of his grandson, a lecture and discussion on the grief process may be far more meaningful for him than an introduction to the latest scientific theory. On the other hand, a teacher going through divorce may want to be in the science lecture because he or she has decided that new ideas will help in his or her grief process.

Superintendents and principals who are aware of certain skills their teachers have, need to encourage these teachers to be presenters in other district's staff development. Frequently one word from a principal or superintendent can open the door for those teachers who would like to offer their consulting skills in a part-time way. The payoff for this is increased esteem all around. All professionals need to be encouraged to become all that they want to become. Finally, in-service and staff development must be open to all the staff. The lunacy of the pecking order needs to end. Offering training to the person lowest on the totem pole helps that person become more than he or she is. If he or she left the school or district as a result of new skills acquired in in-service, educators ought to applaud, for here is a person who through education and learning, has led him- or herself out to a place of betterment, which is the goal of education.

9

Networking for Cooperation

Our Interdependent and Interconnected World

To try to go it alone today is indeed sad. We are already in a new age of cooperation, we have heightened our awareness in the areas of interdependence and interconnectedness. We have recognized for quite some time the universality of all beings on the planet. What Marshal McLuhan and Alvin Toffler have told us is true: we are a global village, and we are in future shock. Bhopal, Chernobyl, and Three Mile Island are known around the world; one country's fossil fuel is another's acid rain, just as one person's energy can tip the balance for a whole community. We are a world community of networkers, and everything we do has an effect upon every one of us and all of the creation. No one is born, no one dies, without it affecting all of us.

We have not always been taught to think this way; often we have been taught to think just the opposite. We like to believe we are "self-made people," but that is not so. Nor is our theme song totally "I Did It My Way." Americans particularly want to believe this, but it is only a legend. We sprang from two people, from a large support group of family and friends, and from the past twenty billion years of the earth; we cannot exist only by ourselves, we need each other, and we need the earth. As we begin to think more clearly, we will come to see that the interconnectedness spoken of throughout this book is indeed true. Educators are far more interconnected than they may have thought or believed.

TRANSFORMING EDUCATION

Cooperation and a cooperative spirit is what makes education work: people cooperating to pay their taxes, teachers cooperating to teach, parents cooperating in believing in the schools and in sending their children there, the children themselves cooperating in participating in school, and on and on. It only works because of everyone; it could not work without global and community resources acting as the town pump from which people drink.

Utilizing Global and Community Resources

Resources range from the community to worldwide. Certainly the Waldorf Schools are global resources for all educators. Recently Joseph Chilton Pearce said there are only two educational approaches really making a difference in the world; one is Sr. Grace Pilon's *Workshop Way* and the other is Waldorf education.[1] Waldorf education is comprehensive, is magnificent at understanding the "art of education" and the development of children, is interconnected and integrated, and has an excellent proven track record in offering freedom, self-responsibility, and a living story to students. Parents play a unique role in the school, and the teachers and parents co-design a Waldorf School. It is interested in whole-brain education and operates with the highest degree of integrity. Rudolf Steiner believed so strongly that education is a drawing out that he allowed all of his work to be used and copied by anyone worldwide. Any educator in the United States who does not know of Dr. Steiner and his schools and colleges is missing a great deal. Any college school of education that does not use some of his ideas and philosophy may indeed be part of the problems in education. There are over three hundred Waldorf Schools worldwide; over eighty in America in more than twenty-five states and the District of Columbia. There is a Waldorf School for mentally disabled adults in Camp Hill, Pennsylvania, and a Teaching College near Sacramento, California.

The *Workshop* Way has already been spoken about in chapter 5. It is being used in over ten countries and is presently being used from pre-school to university across America. It is an educational system which is also a learning process, designed from and based on the principles of psychology. It enables the creation of a new and dynamic environment inside the classroom so that all learning can be creative and students can grow in human skills. It allows all students to discover feelings of importance and intelligence, and the power of self-management of their school day, all day, everyday. In many classes in American schools using Workshop Way there are frequent days of 100% attendance.[2] The main office is in New Orleans, Louisiana, where workshops and college classes are held at Xavier University.

There are other resources and schools also making a difference in education. Some that should be mentioned are the Robert Muller School in Arlington, Texas, the Adlerian-based Sunwood Academy, a school for individual education, in Melbourne, Florida, and the alternative learning centers — many attached to the public school system — across the country.

Keep in mind also that the universe and our deeply mysterious planet earth are themselves great resources and learning laboratories. Whatever it is that education seeks to do must be done in harmony with the universe, in harmony with the planets, in balance with the planet earth. Without this harmony and balance, humans will always be wrong. Meister Eckhart makes two vital points which apply to educators, parents, and students. First, "God is creating the entire universe fully and totally in this present now."[3] This means that education must stop setting up sides in issues and begin to embrace the dialectic, the "both/and." It has already been mentioned that to fail to talk about mystery — a God, a birth, a death — is to leave out the guts of living. To be able to tap into the global and community resources available to all requires that we see the entire universe being recreated every moment. This present now is different from the one that just passed, different from the one that will be here in another moment. Life is not static, it is dynamic; and every living, breathing part of creation has its story to tell, its light to shed upon our dilemmas, frustrations, and joys. We need to be willing to ponder the mystery, to let go enough so that we can plumb the depths, to find first feeling, then knowledge, and then through another letting go, to find wisdom.

Eckhart's second point is this: "When one has learned to let go and let be, then one is well disposed, and he or she is always in the right place whether in society or in solitude. But if one has a wrong attitude, one is always in the wrong place whether in society or not."[4] It is hard to let one's environment be a resource when one is frustrated or has an agenda for another or others. Educators have to answer the call of cooperation and look with the eyes of the children they invite to their schools, to see that which they have *never* seen before. They need to marvel, they need to wonder, they need to allow peak experiences into their lives. Not having this openness means that they will have a wrong attitude, which guarantees that they will be in the wrong place "whether in society or not."

Educators who are well-disposed toward society can utilize global and community resources. They have a willingness to think outrageously, to go with the flow, to let learning flourish. I am reminded of a time when several presidential candidates and the then-President Nixon came to a town to attend the funeral of a very important and influential congressman. School was not only in session, but stayed in session and only those students who through either themselves or their parents, or because of a joint decision, decided they were strong enough to seek out their own education, attended the historic occasion. For the rest of the school a great opportunity for learning was missed.

This is what is meant by "utilizing" the resources. It is much more educational to make history than to read about it, far more educational to participate than to be passive. The forests speak out, the oceans beckon, the sky calls us forth, the plants want to share their story, the mind of the universe is open to all of us, the planet wants to instruct. Educators, through their methods and their content, can either open wide the doors to this wonder or narrow the doorways to offer only a partial view which they can then control. Each answer to a question should call up other questions, and ultimately "Why?" — which can never be answered — will continue to allure us and bring us anew into the circle.

Acknowledgments

To begin, the universe in all its mystery and beauty must be acknowledged; leisure, too, which gave me the ability to contemplate the divine and to learn more about what it is like to be human; allurement, which enabled me to be able to respond to the call to fall in love with all of creation; and to religion, which brought me in touch with the Source.

To all my clients, students, and colleagues — who have really been my teachers — to those who empowererd me through conversation and encouragement, Lois Henningsen; Jean and Bill Shields; Jenai; Matt Fox; Brian Swimme; and especially Charlotte Shields, who consistently encouraged me; Rick Werhli, who taught me to expand my trust; Madeline Cowls, SBS, who believed in me from the very beginning; Santa Maria Roebling, who accepted me unconditionally; Charlie Woodward, who was a model for me in my youth; my parents, who gave me birth; and to the Source of the air which we all breathe, I am grateful.

Notes

Introduction

1. *U.S.A. Today,* Mar. 2, 1987, p 1 D.

Chapter 1

1. Cf. Grace H. Pilon, SBS, *Peace of Mind at an Early Age* (New York: Vantage Press, 1978).

2. Frederick Turner, *Beyond Geography: The Western Spirit Against the Wilderness* (New Jersey: Rutgers University Press, 1983), p. 255.

3. José A. Arguelles, *The Transformative Vision* (Berkeley, CA: Shambhala, 1975), p. 8.

4. Willis Harmon and Howard Rheingold, *Higher Creativity* (Los Angeles: Jeremy P. Tarcher, 1984), p. 71.

5. Abraham H. Maslow, *The Farther Reaches of Human Nature* (New York: Penguin Books, 1976), p. 156.

6. Ibid, p. 158.

7. This phenomenon shows that when enough of us are aware of something, all of us become aware of it. Cf. Ken Keyes, Jr., *The Hundredth Monkey*, 2nd ed. (Coos Bay, Oregon: Vision Books, 1984).

8. José A. Arguelles, op. cit., p. 15.

9. *Contra Costa Times,* Contra Costa County, CA, Dec. 14, 1985, p. 1.

10. John Holt, *Teach Your Own* (New York: Delta/Seymour Lawrence, 1982), p. 168.

11. Erich Jantsch, *The Self-Organizing Universe* (New York: Pergamon Press, 1980), p. 51.

12. John S. Rigden, "The Art of Great Science," *Phi Delta Kappan,* Bloomington, IN, Vol. 64, No. 9, May 1983, p. 615.

13. Ibid.

14. Ibid.

15. Ibid.

16. Erich Jantsch, op. cit., p. 176.

17. Abraham H. Maslow, op. cit., p. 164.

18. Ibid., p. 173.

19. John Holt, *How Children Learn,* Revised Edition (New York: Delta/Seymour Lawrence, 1983), pp. 297-298.

20. Starhawk, *Dreaming The Dark: Magic, Sex & Politics* (Boston: Beacon Press, 1982), p. 136.

21. Lewis Thomas, *The Lives of a Cell* (New York: Bantam Books, 1975), p. 122.

22. Ernest Becker, cited in Matthew Fox, *A Spirituality Named Compassion* (Minneapolis: Winston Press, 1979), p. 193.

23. Matthew Fox, ibid., p. 207.

24. Karen Horney, cited in Matthew Fox, ibid., p. 209.

25. Matthew Fox, ibid.

26. Wendell Berry, *Standing by Words* (San Francisco: North Point Press, 1983), p. 41.

27. Matthew Fox, op. cit., p. 210.

Chapter 2

1. Galileo, cited in Jack Canfield and Harold C. Wells, *100 Ways to Enchance Self-Concept in the Classroom* (New Jersey: Prentice-Hall, 1976), p. 169.

2. Carl Rogers, *On Personal Power* (New York: Dell Publishing Co., 1977), p. 69.

3. Paulo Freire, *Pedagogy of the Oppressed* (New York: Continuum, 1984), p. 61.

4. Ibid., p. 78.

5. John O. Stevens, cited in Canfield and Wells, op. cit., p. 145.

6. Neil Postman and Charles Weingartner, *The School Book* (New York: Dell Publishing, 1973), p. 33.

7. Thomas Carlyle, cited in Canfield and Wells, op. cit., p. 102.

8. Paulo Freire, op. cit., p. 67.

9. Paulo Freire, *Education for Critical Consciousness* (New York: Continuum, 1973), p. 153.

10. Ibid., p. 127.

11. Rosemary Ruether, cited in Matthew Fox, *Original Blessing* (Santa Fe: Bear & Co., 1983), p. 257.

12. John Holt, op. cit., p. 187.

13. Alfred North Whitehead, cited in Matthew Fox, *op. cit.* p. 188.

14. Contributed by a teacher in the midwest.

15. Starhawk, op. cit., p. 138.

16. Cf. Henry Adams, *Mont-Saint-Michel and Chartres* (Princeton, New Jersey: Princeton Univ. Press, 1981).

17. Letter, Iowa Assn. For Supervision and Curriculum Development, 5/3/83.

18. Henry Barnes, a talk at San Francisco Waldorf School, 1/9/86.

19. "A Nation at Risk," a report of the National Commission on Excellence in Education, Special Supplement: The Reports, *DPI Dispatch*, Des Moines, Iowa Department of Public Instruction, Vol. 13, No. 1, September 1983, p. 1.

20. Margaret Mead speaks to this point, see chapter 5.

21. *DPI Dispatch*, p. 1.

22. Ibid., p. 4.

23. Ibid., p. 1.

24. Dwight Allen, an address to the Iowa Association of Lifelong Learning, Des Moines, IA, 10/6/83.

25. *DPI Dispatch,* p. 1.

26. Ibid.

27. Ibid., p. 2.

28. Ibid.

29. Ibid.

30. Ibid.

31. Ibid.

32. Ibid.

33. Ibid., p. 3.

34. Ibid.

35. Ibid.

36. "A Nation at Risk," An Open Letter by the Iowa Association for Supervision and Curriculum Development, Cedar Falls, IA, April, 1983, p. 16.

37. Ibid.

38. *DPI Dispatch,* p. 3.

39. Ibid.

40. Ibid.

41. Wendell Berry, *op. cit.,* p. 41.

42. *DPI Dispatch,* p. 4.

43. Ibid.

44. Ibid.

45. Ibid.

46. Ibid.

47. Ibid., pp. 5-7.

48. Ibid., p. 6.

Chapter 3

1. José A. Arguelles, op. cit., p. 4.

2. Ruth Nanda Ashen, cited in Ivan Illich, *Deschooling Society* (New York: Harper Colophon, 1983), pp. 178-179

3. John Holt, *How Children Learn,* p. ix.

4. Rollo May, in a talk at the Institute in Culture and Creation Spirituality, Holy Names College, Oakland, Ca., 4/10/85.

5. Gene Marine, in *Express,* The East Bay's Free Weekly, Express Publishing Co., Berkeley, CA, 7/19/85, p. 1.

6. Pablo Casals, cited in Matthew Fox, *Original Blessing,* p. 43.

7. Matthew Fox, *Meditations with Meister Eckhart* (Santa Fe: Bear & Co., 1982), p. 14.

8. Josef Pieper, *Leisure: the Basis of Culture* (New York: Pantheon, 1952), p. i.

9. Plato, cited in Josef Pieper, ibid., p. 19.

10. Cited in Josef Pieper, ibid., p. 19.

11. Josef Pieper, ibid.

12. Dick Gregory, cited in Matthew Fox, *Original Blessing,* p. 67.

13. Starhawk, op. cit., p. 11.

14. Josef Pieper, op. cit., p. 20.

15. Thomas Aquinas, cited in Josef Pieper, ibid., p. 31.

16. Josef Pieper, ibid., pp.32-33.

17. Brian Swimme, *The Universe is a Green Dragon* (Santa Fe: Bear & Co., 1985), p. 47.

18. Ibid., p. 48.

19. *Webster's New World Dictionary of the American Language,* Second College Edition, ed. by David B. Guralink (New York: Simon and Schuster, 1984), p. 1217.

20. Matthew Fox, "Recycling the three R's," *Creation,* Vol. 1, No. 1, Oakland, CA, March/April 1985, p. 14.

21. Robert Muller, *New Genesis* (New York: Image Books, 1984), p. 37.

22. Webster's, op. cit., p. 1203.

23. Ibid., p. 1211.

24. Matthew Fox, "Recycling the three R's," loc. cit., p. 15.

25. Albert Einstein, cited in Matthew Fox, *Original Blessing*, p. 66.

26. Mary Caroline Richards, *The Public School and the Education of the Whole Person* (New York: Pilgrim Press, 1980), p. 5.

27. Frederick Turner. op. cit., 25.

28. Brian Swimme, op. cit., p. 75.

29. Thomas Berry, "The Earth Community," *Riverdale Papers,* (New York: Riverdale Center For Religious Research), Vol. VIII, pp. 5-6.

30. Matthew Fox, *Original Blessing*, p. 72.

31. Andrew Weil, *The Natural Mind* (Boston: Houghton Mifflin, 1972), p. 179.

32. Thomas Berry, "Our Children: Their Future," *Riverdale Papers,* Vol IX, 1982, p. 2

33. Thomas Berry, "The New Story," *Riverdale Papers,* Vol. V, p. 2.

34. Gregory Bateson, *Steps to an Ecology of Mind* (New York: Ballantine Books, 1972), p. 434.

Chapter 4

1. Leroy G. Baruth and Daniel G. Eckstein, *The ABC'S of Classroom Discipline* (Dubuque: Kendall/Hunt, 1978), p. 76.

2. Sam Keen, *To a Dancing God* (New York: Harper & Row, 1970), pp. 60-61.

3. René M. Querido, *Creativity in Education: The Waldorf Approach* (San Francisco: H. S. Dakin Co., 1982), p. 1.

4. Robert J. Keeshan, "The Nurturing of Young America," an address given at the Fourth Governor's Conference on Education For Parenthood, Kansas State Univ., Manhattan, KS, Mar. 17, 1984, p. 5.

5. Don Dinkmeyer, Sr., Don Dinkmeyer, Jr., and Gary D. McKay, *Systematic Training for Effective Teaching (STET)*, Teacher's Handbook (Circle Pines, MN: American Guidance Service, 1980), p. 7.

6. Jean Liedloff, *The Continuum Concept* (New York: Warner Communications, 1979), pp. 209-210.

7. Don Dinkmeyer, Sr., Don Dinkmeyer, Jr., and Gary D. McKay, op. cit., p. 182.

8. Carl Rogers, op. cit., pp. 69-70.

9. Robert D. Myrick and Tom Erney, *Caring and Sharing: Becoming a Peer Facilitator* (Minneapolis: Educational Media Corp., 1978), p. 9.

10. Ardyth Hebeisen, *Peer Program for Youth* (Minneapolis: Augsburg Publishing House, 1973), p.5.

11. Sid Simon has a warm and wonderful little book on this subject: *I am Lovable and Capable (ILAC)* (Niles, IL: Argus Communications, 1973).

12. Naomi White, "I Taught Them All" (reprinted from *Progressive Education,* Nov. 1943), cited in Jack Canfield and Harold C. Wells, op. cit., p. 201.

13. Pablo Casals, cited in Matthew Fox, *Original Blessing,* p. 94.

14. Jean Liedloff, op. cit., p. 213.

15. Rudolf Dreikurs, cited in Leroy G. Baruth and Daniel G. Eckstein, op. cit., p. 76.

16. Donald E. Hamacek, cited in Jack Canfield and Harold C. Wells, op. cit., p. 104.

17. Rudolf Dreikurs, M.D., and Vicki Stolz, R.N., *Children the Challenge* (New York: Hawthorn/Dutton, 1964), p. 36.

18. Ibid., pp. 38-39.

19. I am indebted to Starhawk, op. cit., p. 78, for this idea.

20. Art Buchwald, "Love and the Cabbie," cited in Jack Canfield and Harold C. Wells, op. cit., pp. 19-20.

21. Robert J. Keeshan, op. cit., pp. 2-3.

22. Urie Bronfenbrenner, cited in "Curricula For Caring: Overcoming the Alienation of the Young," by Timothy V. Rasinski, in *The Journal of Humanistic Education and Development,* Vol. 23, No. 2, Dec. 1984, p. 89.

23. Sam Keen, op. cit., p. 43.

24. Ibid.

25. Ibid.

26. Ibid., p. 45.

27. Matthew Fox, *Original Blessing,* p. 135.

28. Ibid., p. 136.

29. Sam Keen, op. cit., pp. 49-50.

30. Matthew Fox, *Original Blessing,* p. 137.

31. Brian Swimme, op. cit., p. 120.

32. Ivan Illich, *Deschooling Society* (New York: Harper Colophon, 1983), p. 35.

33. John Holt, *Teach Your Own,* p. 149.

34. Mary Caroline Richards, cited in Matthew Fox, *A Spirituality Named Compassion,* p. 104.

35. Sue Spayth Riley, *How to Generate Values in Young Children* (Washington, DC: National Assn. For The Education Of Young Children, 1984), p. 55.

36. A. S. Neill, cited in Herb Snitzer, *Living at Summerhill* (New York: Collier Books, 1968), p. 10.

37. Sue Spayth Riley, op. cit., p. 63.

38. John Holt, *How Children Learn,* p. 293.

39. Sue Spayth Riley, op. cit., p. 53.

40. Rollo May, *The Courage to Create* (New York: Bantam Books, 1980), p. vii.

41. Neil Postman and Charles Weingartner, *op. cit.,* p. 134.

42. Sam Keen, op. cit., p. 41.

43. Matthew Fox, *A Spirituality Named Compassion,* p. 4.

44. Norman Cousins, *Anatomy of an Illness as Perceived by the Patient* (New York: Bantam Books, 1981).

45. Lewis Thomas, op. cit., p. 98.

46. Donald E. Hammacek, loc. cit.

47. H. Stephen Glenn, *Strengthening the Family,* ed. by Carol Marcus and Jean McMillen (privately printed, Washington, DC: Potomac Press, 1981), p. 6.

48. Ibid.

49. Stephen Glenn, "Strategies & Self Esteem," a talk delivered at Cedar Falls, IA, March 2, 1984.

50. Ibid.

51. Sue Spayth Riley, op. cit., p. 7.

52. A. S. Neill, cited in Herb Snitzer, op. cit., p. 9.

53. Viola Spolin, cited in Jack Canfield and Harold C. Wells, op. cit., p. 138.

54. Peter M. Kalellis, *On the Other Hand . . . Deciding What to do About Indecision* (Allen, TX: Argus, 1980), p. 51.

55. Don Dinkmeyer, Sr., Don Dinkmeyer, Jr., and Gary D. McKay, op. cit., p. 7.

56. A. S. Neill, cited in Herb Snitzer, op. cit., p. 9.

57. Clark Moustakas, cited in Sue Spayth Riley, op. cit., p. 16.

58. Jean Liedloff, op. cit., pp. 140, 142.

59. Don Dinkmeyer, Sr., Don Dinkmeyer, Jr., and Gary D. McKay, op. cit., p. 13.

60. John Holt, *How Children Learn,* p. 290.

61. Sue Spayth Riley, op. cit., p. 37.

Chapter 5

1. René M. Querido, op. cit., p. 15.

2. Anthony F. Gregorc and Helen B. Ward, "A New Definition For Individual," *NASSP Bulletin* (Reston, VA: National Assn. of Secondary School Principals), Feb. 1977, pp. 20-26.

3. Gregory Bateson, *Mind and Nature* (New York: Bantam, 1979), pp. 6-7.

4. Paulo Freire, *Pedagogy of the Oppressed,* p. 97.

5. Ibid., p. 98.

6. David Keirsey and Marilyn Bates, *Please Understand Me* (Del Mar, CA: Prometheus Nemesis, 1984), p. 100.

7. Ibid., p. 166.

8. Grace H. Pilon, SBS, op. cit., p. 40.

9. Ibid., p. 1.

10. Ibid., p. 4.

11. Grace H. Pilon, SBS, "The Workshop, A Better Way," *Early Years*, Sept. 1970, p. 105.

12. Ibid.

13. Don Dinkmeyer, Sr., Don Dinkmeyer, Jr., and Gary D. McKay, op. cit., pp. 246-247.

14. *Handicapped Students and Special Education* (Rosemont, MN: Data Research, 1985), p. 1.

15. Don Dinkmeyer, Sr., Don Dinkmeyer, Jr., and Gary D. McKay, op. cit., p. 246.

16. Ibid., p. 258.

17. I am indebted to Miryam Regele for this term.

18. Don Dinkmeyer, Sr., Don Dinkmeyer, Jr., and Gary D. McKay, op. cit., p. 246.

19. Ibid.

20. Linnus Pecaut, cited in Don Dinkmeyer, Sr., Don Dinkmeyer, Jr., and Gary D. McKay, op. cit., p. 252.

21. Ibid.

22. Ibid., p. 255.

23. Ibid., p. 257.

Chapter 6

1. Robert Muller, op. cit., p. 53.

2. Ibid., p. 52.

3. Brian Swimme, op. cit., p. 73.

NOTES TO PAGES 112-119

4. Ibid., p. 74.

5. Calvin DeWitt, "The Au Sable Institute: A New Venture In Creation Consciousness," cited in *Cry of the Environment,* ed. by Philip N. Joranson and Ken Butigan (Santa Fe: Bear & Co., 1984), p. 449.

6. Robert Muller, op. cit., p. 7.

7. *John F. Kennedy on Education,* ed. by William T. O'Hara (New York: Teachers College Press, Columbia Univ., 1965), pp. 10-11.

8. Margaret Mead, cited in "Responding To The Economic Sputnik," by Phyllis Marcuccio, *Phi Delta Kappan,* op. cit., p. 618.

9. Robert Muller, op. cit., p. 124.

10. Marilyn Ferguson, *The Aquarian Conspiracy* (Los Angeles: J. P. Tarcher, 1980), p. 306.

11. Teilhard de Chardin, cited in Matthew Fox, *Original Blessing,* p. 66.

12. Gregory Bateson, *Mind and Nature,* p. 8.

13. Marilyn Ferguson, op. cit., p. 303.

14. Mary Caroline Richards, *Toward Wholeness: Rudolf Steiner Education in America* (Middletown, CT: Wesleyan Univ. Press, 1980), pp. 63-64.

15. Rudolf Steiner, cited in Mary Caroline Richards, op. cit., p. 65.

16. Erich Jantsch, op. cit., p. xiii.

17. Robert Muller, op. cit., p. 7.

18. Adapted from Robert Muller, Ibid., pp. 140-155.

19. Cited in Matthew Fox, "The Case For Extrovert Meditation," *Spirituality Today,* June 1978, p. 165.

20. Ibid., p. 167.

21. Mary Caroline Richards, cited in Matthew Fox, Ibid., p. 171.

22. Ibid., p. 174.

23. Matthew Fox, *A Spirituality Named Compassion,* p. 3.

24. Ibid., p. 220.

25. Don Dinkmeyer and Gary D. McKay, *Systematic Training For Effective Parenting* (Circle Pines, MN: American Guidance Service, 1976)

26. Robert Muller, op. cit., p. 22.

27. Ernst Buhler, cited in William Jordan, "Waldorf Education in State Schools," *Child and Man: Education as an Art,* (England: Steiner Schools Fellowship), Vol. 19, No. 2, Summer, 1985, p. 10.

28. René M. Querido, op. cit., p. 1.

29. Warren Ashe, Roland Everett, Alan Hall, Chris Marshall, Brien Masters, "What Are Schools For," *Child and Man: Education as an Art,* op. cit., p. 15.

30. Ibid., p. 16.

31. René M. Querido, op. cit., p. 5.

32. Ibid.

33. Ibid.

34. A. S. Neill, cited in Herb Snitzer, op. cit., p. 10.

35. Rudolf Steiner, *The Curriculum of the First Waldorf School,* tr. by Eileen Hutchins (England: Steiner Schools Fellowship, 1966), p. 29.

36. Ivan Illich, op. cit., p. 135.

37. Ibid., p. 143.

38. Rudolf Steiner, op. cit., p. 39.

39. Ibid.

40. Ibid., p. 41.

41. Ibid., p. 45.

42. Ibid.

43. Ibid., p. 31.

44. Ibid., p. 42.

45. Ibid., p. 32.

46. Cited in John Holt, *Teach Your Own,* p. 72-73.

47. Brian Swimme, op. cit., p. 95.

48. Cited in John Holt, op. cit., pp. 173-174.

49. Ibid., p. 175.

50. Ibid., p. 176.

51. Ibid., pp. 180-181.

52. Ibid., p. 182.

53. Ibid., pp. 181-183.

54. Ibid., p. 183.

55. Neil Postman and Charles Weingartner, op. cit., p. 115.

56. John Holt, op. cit., p. 73.

57. Ibid., pp. 73-74.

58. David A. Squires, William G. Huitt and John K. Segars, *Effective Schools and Classrooms: A Research Based Perspective* (Alex., VA: Assn. for Supervision And Curriculum Development, 1983).

59. Ibid., p. 2.

60. Ibid., p. 3.

61. Ibid.

Chapter 7

1. Marilyn Ferguson, op. cit., p. 201.

2. James MacGregor Burns, cited in Marilyn Ferguson, op. cit., p. 202.

3. Marilyn Ferguson, op. cit., p. 202.

4. Thomas J. Peters and Robert H. Waterman, Jr., *In Search of Excellence: Lessons from America's Best-Run Companies* (New York: Harper & Row, 1982), p. 74.

5. Marilyn Ferguson, op. cit., p. 208.

6. John Naisbitt, *Megatrends* (New York: Warner Books, 1982), p. 101.

7. Ibid., p. 188.

8. Thomas J. Peters and Robert H. Waterman, op. cit., pp. 74-75.

9. James MacGregor Burns, cited in Marilyn Ferguson, op. cit., p. 208.

10. Charles C. Hardy, "The best teaching is just plain hard work," *San Francisco Examiner,* Dec. 9, 1985, p. A6.

11. Ibid., pp. A1, A6.

12. Raj K. Chopra, *Making a Bad Situation Good* (Nashville: Thomas Nelson Publishers, 1984), p. 8.

13. James MacGregor Burns, cited in Thomas J. Peters and Robert H. Waterman, Jr., op. cit., p. 83.

14. Raj K. Chopra, op. cit., Contents page.

15. Tom Hayden, cited in Marilyn Ferguson, op. cit., p. 209.

16. Adapted from Marilyn Ferguson, op. cit., pp. 210-212.

Chapter 8

1. John E. Penick and Robert E. Yager, "The Search For Excellence In Science Education," *Phi Delta Kappan,* p. 622.

2. Howard Kirschenbaum, Sidney B. Simon, Rodney W. Napier, *Wad-Ja-Get? The Grading Game in American Education* (New York: Hart Publishing, 1971), p. 23.

3. Scripps-Howard News Service, "Despite cheating scandal, Stanford stands by its honor system," *San Francisco Examiner,* Dec. 25, 1985, p. B2.

4. Howard Kirschenbaum, Sidney B. Simon, Rodney W. Napier, op. cit., p. 24.

5. Studs Terkel, cited in David Keirsey and Marilyn Bates, op. cit., p. 46.

6. Howard Kirschenbaum, Sidney B. Simon, Rodney W. Napier, op. cit., p. 23.

7. Ibid., pp. 23-24.

8. Ibid., p. 24.

9. Ibid.

10. Ivan Illich, op. cit., p. 108.

11. Raj K. Chopra, op. cit., p. 19.

12. John Holt, op. cit., pp. 340-341.

13. Ibid.

14. Ibid., p. 343.

Chapter 9

1. Joseph Chilton Pearce, a talk at St. Mary's College, Moraga, CA, Feb. 28, 1986.

2. Grace H. Pilon, SBS, op. cit., p. 61.

3. Matthew Fox, *Meditations with Meister Eckhart,* p. 26.

4. Ibid., p. 63.

Glossary

Allurement

The power of attraction or fascination; of being enchanted with something. "Following one's allurement" means following what one is attracted to. It is a way that is effortless.

Art as Meditation

An activity which wakes up the inner core of one's being through letting go and wonder; it allows creativity to flow. An example of painting as meditation would be to meditate on an object, close one's eyes, and sketch or paint the object. Art as meditation is oriented toward process; it does not have an object (the painting) as its goal.

Banking Approach to Education

The belief that education is made up of fixed ideas or a fixed content which are "taught" by a "superior" (teacher), and which must be "learned" by the "inferior" (student). The banking approach questions little, accepts what "experts" say, and believes that schools are banks which hold a deposit of knowledge which all students must receive in the same degree and preferably with the same intensity. Using this approach, neither teachers nor students critically observe reality.

Beauty

The good which exists in the universe, and which extends to people and societies. It gives pleasure to the senses, and pleasurably exalts the mind and the spirit. It exists especially in nature and natural things, in the depths, and in quiet.

Bioregion

A geographic area of the self-organizing earth in which land, sea, and air, including plant, animal, and human life participate. Bioregions are self-educating, self-governing, self-healing, self-fulfilling, self-propagating, and self-nourishing communities.

Celebration

Honoring the universe and all its creation through festivals, ceremonies, and rites; "a forgetting of ego, of problems, of difficulties in order to remember," says Matthew Fox. The Jewish word for celebration *kagiyaah* means to draw a circle, or go round. Many ethnic celebrations consist of circle dances, and folkdancing usually takes place "drawing a circle."

Compassion/Justice-Making

From the Latin *cum patior,* it means to stand with, to be in solidarity with. It does not mean to pity, nor to be sentimental. People who are compassionate stand with others in their travail; furthermore, they do something about helping to change the structures which keep justice from happening.

Consumerism

Consumerism is really two things: it is the rampart buying of goods and services, but it is also the belief that through the securing of these goods and services, people will psychologically become happy. "Packaged substitutes for feeling, sold at a profit to a mass market," says Starhawk.

Cosmos

The primary revelation of all life and self-organization; an orderly, harmonious, systematic universe. The universe in contrast to the earth alone, characterized by greatness, intensity, and comprehensiveness.

Culture

What individuals become when they coalesce into a group, a nation, a people, and develop a history. Culture makes them one and supports their world view or pattern of behaving. Culture also refers to a people's customary beliefs, social forms, and material traits. "There is a tendency," says Lewis Thomas, "for living things to join up, establish linkages, live inside each other, return to earlier arrangements, get along whenever possible. This is the way of the world."

Descartes/Cartesian World View

Scientific laws posited by Descartes in 1619 claimed, among other things, that truth must be clearly known; that anything under examination must be divided into its greatest number of parts; and that reviews should be so general that one could be assured that nothing was omitted. He is the father of modern rationalism. "I think, therefore I am," led the scientific community to define the human as a "rational animal." His world view is dualistic; it helped to separate and to pit science and religion against each other for over 350 years.

Dialectic

Systematic reasoning which juxtaposes opposed or contradictory ideas and works to resolve their conflict by a new synthesis.

Dialogue

Listening with understanding, using the ears *and* the heart. Dialogue presupposes equality of persons, and a connection between them and their world, and their problems and joys. Dialogue provides each other with true thoughts, feelings, intentions, and actions.

Differently-abled

A new term which recognizes that although humans are members of one species, each is unique. It affirms a person's uniqueness while at the same time not masking or denying difference.

Dualism

Conceiving ideas in an "either/or" framework, as opposed to the whole, the "both/and." Dualism not only causes the taking of sides, but it presupposes the viewing of the opposite side in an adversarial way, which precludes uniqueness and leads to dichotomy, separation, and alienation.

Education

From the Latin *educare* which means to draw out; to lead out. It also means to spend time. Hence, education means to draw out from students that which is in their minds and hearts. It also means spending time with students, even as Sam Keen says, "wasting time" with them.

Education as Art

The ability to view education in a holistic, process-oriented way; a "drawing out" of that which is inside each individual student. This view both opens the student to the wisdom of the world and accepts his or her unique interpretation of that world. Its goal is to help the student become the best person he or she can become. It is interested in developing both the character of the student and the beauty of the universe and ideas, as well as an understanding of how the universe and ideas work. It is an educational method which aims at fitting things together, seeing their interrelationships.

Education as Industry

A systematic approach which views education as cause and effect: orderly, conforming, and predictable. It deals mainly with a product, has little interest in the process, and holds to the belief that figures and statistics are more important than children's development and the development of their values.

Empathy

The ability to see the world as another perceives it, from their "internal frame of reference," without losing one's own identity or objectivity.

Encouragement

A process of the heart which helps students believe in themselves and in their abilities. It is not an earned achievement but is a positive attitude of being with others. Any movement at all can be encouraged, no matter how small or insignificant. It focuses on the work or effort, and treats students with acceptance and respect. It also helps them develop the courage to be imperfect. Encouraging teachers are asset finders rather than fault finders.

Ethics/Morals

Ethics is a discipline which deals with the good and the principles, values, and customs which flow from that good. Morals refers to the behavior which conforms to ethical standards.

Holiness

The ability to perceive the cosmos within the human personality and within all of creation. It is not a separation of humanity and divinity, but a coming together of both in creation.

Holism/Wholeness

A way of understanding the universe and nature from the perspective of interconnectedness and interacting wholes that are more than the mere sum of elementary particles. It emphasizes the organic relation between parts and wholes.

Inclusive

Broad in orientation or scope; openness to what is; that which offers diversity, excitement, differentiation, and thus increased learning. The opposite is exclusive, which separates, closes off, shuts out, and bars from participation or consideration.

Integration

Incorporation as equals into a society or group of individuals; a fitting together characterized by acceptance.

Interconnectedness

The bonding which comes about by making a connection.

Interdependent

A mutual dependence in which the parties both feed on and are fed, lean on, and are leaned upon. Interdependent parties manifest both independence and a willingness to get along with others.

Intrinsic

That which is within, which belongs to the essential nature of a thing or person.

Leisure

The art of silence and insight which issues forth in non-activity. It is a type of "day-dreaming" which recharges the human batteries. Plato defined leisure as the contemplation of nature and of God. It is nourishment for the human soul, a celebration of gratitude and joyfulness to the divine at being selected to dine at the cosmic table.

Macrocosm/Microcosm

Macrocosm refers to a great world, the universe, that which is exceptionally large, a global umbrella. Microcosm refers to that which is very small, usually subsumed within the macrocosm.

Mentor

Originally, a friend of Odysseus entrusted with the education of Odysseus' son Telemachus; hence, a trusted counselor or guide, tutor or coach.

Nationalism

Loyalty and devotion to a nation which is so strong that there is a sense of national consciousness exalting one nation above all others. It places primary emphasis on promotion of its culture and interests as opposed to those of other nations or supranational groups.

Nation At Risk

A report from the 18-member panel called the National Commission on Excellence in Education. Created in 1981, its mission was the reform of public education.

Paradigm

A shift in archetypes which comes about from the reaching of critical mass; a breakout, a breakthrough which encompasses whole populations or species. Man walking upright is an example.

Pathology

The structural and functional changes produced in an organism by disease.

Patriarchy

Cultural and social organization marked by the supremacy of the father in the clan or the family, the legal dependence of wives and children, and the reckoning of the descent and inheritance in the male line. By extension, this term refers to a male-dominated society, in which women and children are second class citizens.

Personal Maturity

The process of becoming honest and self-responsible. Unlike physical maturity, which happens during late adolescence, personal maturity happens only when one decides to make it happen. There are four stages in personal maturity; infancy, childhood, adolescence, and adulthood. Adulthood is characterized by demonstrating the ability to be honest consistently, to make choices freely, and to accept consequences for those choices.

Pedagogue

Originally, a pedagogue was the slave who escorted children to school. By extension, it now refers to a teacher or schoolmaster.

Planetism

The teaching that all planetary bodies of the universe are interrelated and interconnected.

Power

From the Latin *posse,* it means to be able. It is an energy that comes from within.

Power-Over

Using power in a dominating way, such as authoritarianism, commanding, domination, supremacy, control, or absolutism.

Power-With

Using power in an efficacious way which leads to empowerment, enablement, and strengthening. It gets learned through trust.

Praxis

Putting thought into action.

Reformation

A straightening out, a restoring; a change for the better, an activity which improves. It refers to changes on the outside, on the periphery. Frequently, administrators who engage in reformation believe they are engaged in transformation. This is not the case. Reformation is analogous to remodeling, where the structure remains the same.

Responsibility

Being accountable for that which has been agreed upon. "Self-responsibility" refers to being in charge of oneself and accepting consequences for one's actions. In the widest sense, one is responsible only for oneself; he or she responds *to* all others. Obviously, educators have some responsibility for young children, but educators' responsibility *for* their students lessens as their students grow in personal maturity.

Reverence

A feeling or attitude of deep respect, love, and awe, as for something sacred.

Ritual

The established form of a ceremony. In education, ritual can take many forms, from the teacher welcoming each student individually each day, to the communal reading of poetry, to temple massage and backrubs, to celebrations of occurrences in nature such as solstice and arbor day, to observances of religious significance such as Passover, Hanukkah, Easter, Christmas.

Shaman

One, usually a priest, who uses magic for curing the sick and divining the hidden.

Self-Esteem

Awareness of confidence and satisfaction in oneself, marked by the knowledge of the presence of these four conditions: a sense of uniqueness, a sense of connectedness with all of creation, a sense of personal power, and an ability to have and learn from role models.

Synergy

A cooperative action in which the total effect or combined benefit is greater than the sum of the effects of benefits taken independently.

Technocracy

Government by technicians; management of society by technical experts.

Transcendence

Beyond limits; participation in the metaworld.

Transforming Leadership

A leadership which engages in such a radical way that both leader and followers are raised to a new level of motivation, morality, and self- and other-responsibility. Their purposes are aligned so completely and understood so clearly that both leader and the led become fused in their desires, and a new power—empowerment— emanates from their relationship. It becomes moral in that it raises the level of human awareness and action, participates more fully in the rhythms of the universe, and affects the ethical conduct of both leader and the led.

Transformation

An act or process which completely changes the composition or structure; that which transfigures, shapes. A change so dramatic that the character or disposition is shaped differently.

Values

From the Latin *valere* meaning to be worth, to be strong. Those ideals which we hold to be significant for our lives. Values get established from an internal mix based on what we have learned from family, school, society, and religion, tempered with choices we make, and beliefs we hold. Some values are lifelong beliefs; other values change as individuals grow and mature.

Waldorf Education

Soon after World War I, Rudolf Steiner, an eminent Austrian educator, was asked to begin a school at the Waldorf Astoria cigarette factory in Stuttgart, Germany. The factory owner was concerned that although the country was rebuilding economically, there was no artistic expression for children. In 1919, Steiner opened this first "Waldorf School" and within six years established six others. Today, Waldorf Education is three hundred schools worldwide—over eighty of them in the United States. There is a Waldorf School for mentally disabled adults in Camp Hill, PA, and a teaching college near Sacramento, CA.

Wonder

The quality of being amazed, astonished, of having awe aroused by something strange, miraculous, mysterious, or new to one's experience; akin to the process of letting go and letting be in which one enters darkness to find light.

Workshop Way

A system of education founded over twenty years ago by Sr. Grace Pilon, SBS, which fosters freedom with responsibility, creativity and openness, and highly regards the learning environment. Learning materials are of a hands-on nature and are usually made by the teacher. Pilon believes the social conditioning of the classroom must be such that it creates many positive relationships among and between students and teachers. Workshop Way is being used from pre-school through university in the United States and in over ten countries around the world.

Bibliography

Arguelles, José A. *The Transformative Vision.* Berkeley, CA: Shambhala, 1975.

Ashe, Warren, Everett, Roland, Hall, Alan, Marshall, Chris, Masters, Brien, "What Are Schools For," *Child and Man: Education as an Art.* England: Steiner Schools Fellowship, Vol. 19, No. 2, Summer, 1985.

Baruth, Leroy G., and Eckstein, Daniel G. *The ABC'S of Classroom Discipline.* Dubuque: Kendall/Hunt, 1978.

Bateson, Gregory. *Steps to an Ecology of Mind.* New York: Ballantine Books, 1972.

_____ *Mind and Nature.* New York: Bantam, 1979.

Berry, Thomas. "The Earth Community." *Riverdale Papers.* New York: Riverdale Center For Religious Research, Vol. VIII, 1982.

_____ "Our Children: Their Future." *Riverdale Papers,* Vol. IX, 1982.

_____ "The New Story." *Riverdale Papers,* Vol. V, 1981.

Berry, Wendell. *Standing by Words.* San Francisco: North Point Press, 1983.

Canfield, Jack, and Wells, Harold C. *100 Ways to Enchance Self-Concept in the Classroom.* New Jersey: Prentice Hall, 1976.

Chopra, Raj, K. *Making a Bad Situation Good.* Nashville: Thomas Nelson Publishers, 1984.

Cousins, Norman. *Anatomy of an Illness as Perceived by the Patient.* New York: Bantam Books, 1981.

Crook, Gloria. *World Core Curriculum Manual.* Arlington, TX: The Robert Muller School, 1986.

Dinkmeyer, Don, and Gary D. McKay, *Systematic Training For Effective Parenting.* Circle Pines, MN: American Guidance Service, 1976.

Dinkmeyer, Don, Sr., Dinkmeyer, Don, Jr., and McKay, Gary, *Systematic Training for Effective Teaching (STET),* Teacher's Handbook. Circle Pines, MN: American Guidance Service, 1980.

Dreikurs, Rudolf, M.D., and Stolz, Vicki, R.N. *Children the Challenge.* New York: Hawthorn/Dutton, 1964.

Ferguson, Marilyn. *The Aquarian Conspiracy.* Los Angeles: J. P. Tarcher, 1980.

Fox, Matthew. *A Spirituality Named Compassion.* Minneapolis: Winston Press, 1979.

———. *Meditations with Meister Eckhart.* Santa Fe: Bear & Co., 1982.

———. *Original Blessing.* Santa Fe: Bear & Co., 1983.

———. The Case For Extrovert Meditation. *Spirituality Today.*

Freire, Paulo. *Education for Critical Consciousness.* New York: Continuum, 1973.

———. *Pedagogy of the Oppressed.* New York: Continuum, 1984.

Glenn, H. Stephen. *Strengthening the Family.* Ed. by Carol Marcus and Jean McMillen. Washington, DC: Potomac Press, 1981.

———. "Strategies & Self Esteem." A talk delivered at Cedar Falls, IA, March 2, 1984.

Harmon, Willis, and Rheingold, Howard. *Higher Creativity.* Los Angeles: Jeremy P. Tarcher, 1984.

Hebeisen, Ardyth. *Peer Program for Youth.* Minneapolis: Augsburg Publishing House, 1973.

Holt, John, *Teach Your Own.* New York: Delta/Seymour Lawrence, 1982.

———. *How Children Learn.* Revised Edition. New York: Delta/Seymour Lawrence, 1983.

BIBLIOGRAPHY

Illich, Ivan. *Deschooling Society.* New York: Harper Colophon, 1971.

Iowa Department of Public Instruction. "A Nation at Risk: A report of the National Commission on Excellence in Education." Special Supplement: The Reports. *DPI Dispatch,* Vol.13, No. 1, September 1983.

Jantsch, Erich. *The Self-Organizing Universe.* New York: Pergamon Press, 1980.

Keen, Sam. *To a Dancing God.* New York: Harper & Row, 1970.

Keeshan, Robert J. "The Nurturing of Young America." An address given at the Fourth Governor's Conference on Education For Parenthood, Kansas State University, Manhattan, KS., Mar. 17, 1984.

Keirsey, David, and Bates, Marilyn. *Please Understand Me.* Del Mar, CA: Prometheus Nemesis, 1984.

Kirschenbaum, Howard, Simon, Sidney B., and Napier, Rodney W. *Wad-Ja-Get? The Grading Game in American Education.* New York: Hart Publishing, 1971.

Liedloff, Jean. *The Continuum Concept.* New York: Warner Communications, 1979.

Maslow, Abraham H. *The Farther Reaches of Human Nature* New York: Penguin Books, 1976.

May, Rollo. *The Courage to Create.* New York: Bantam Books, 1980.

Muller, Robert. *New Genesis.* New York: Image Books, 1984.

Myrick, Robert D., and Erney, Tom. *Caring and Sharing: Becoming a Peer Facilitator.* Minneapolis: Educational Media Corp., 1978.

Naisbitt, John. *Megatrends.* New York: Warner Books, 1982.

Peters, Thomas J. and Waterman, Robert H., Jr.. *In Search of Excellence: Lessons from America's Best-Run Companies.* New York: Harper & Row, 1982.

Pieper, Josef. *Leisure: the Basis of Culture.* New York: Pantheon, 1952.

Pilon, Grace H. SBS. "The Workshop, A Better Way." *Early Years,* Sept. 1970.

———— *Peace of Mind at an Early Age.* New York: Vantage Press, 1978.

Postman, Neil, and Weingartner, Charles. *The School Book.* New York: Dell Publishing, 1973.

Querido, René M. *Creativity in Education: The Waldorf Approach.* San Francisco: H. S. Dakin Co., 1982.

Richards, Mary Caroline. *The Public School and the Education of the Whole Person.* New York: Pilgrim Press, 1980.

———— *Toward Wholeness: Rudolf Steiner Education in America.* Middletown, CT: Wesleyan Univ. Press, 1980.

Rigden, John S. "The Art of Great Science." *Phi Delta Kappan.* Bloomington, IN, Vol. 64, No. 9, May 1983.

Riley, Sue Spayth. *How to Generate Values in Young Children.* Washington, DC: National Assn. For The Education Of Young Children, 1984.

Rogers, Carl. *On Personal Power.* New York: Dell Publishing Co., 1977.

Simon, Sidney B. *I am Loveable and Capable (ILAC).* Niles, IL: Argus Communications, 1973.

Snitzer, Herb. *Living at Summerhill.* New York: Collier Books, 1968.

Starhawk. *Dreaming The Dark: Magic, Sex & Politics.* Boston: Beacon Press, 1982.

Steiner, Rudolf. *The Curriculum of the First Waldorf School.* Tr. by Eileen Hutchins. England: Steiner Schools Fellowship, 1966.

Swimme, Brian. *The Universe is a Green Dragon.* Santa Fe: Bear & Co., 1985.

Thomas, Lewis. *The Lives of a Cell.* New York: Bantam Books, 1975.

Turner, Frederick. *Beyond Geography: The Western Spirit Against the Wilderness.* New Jersey: Rutgers University Press, 1983.

Index

Acceptance, touch, and trust, 63-72
Acid rain, 60
Adler, Alfred, 76, 95, 179
Admiration and encouragement, 72-78
Advertising as aid to consumerism, 17, 18
Alcohol abuse. *See* Drug and alcohol abuse
Alexander the Great, 130
Allen, Dwight, 36
Allurement as part of education, 51-52
"America Can Do It," 44
Ancient civilizations, 48, 49, 130-131, 135
Animals and plants, 112
Anshen, Ruth Nanda, 45
Apollo project, 33
Aquinas, Thomas, 50-51
Arguelles, José A., 6, 9, 45
Art, 45-62, 121
  difference between industry and art, 12-16
  drama, 120, 130
  meditation, art as, 117-118
  See also Culture; Music
Astronauts, 48
Aztec sundial, 48

"Banking approach" to education, 21-27, 38
Barnes, Henry, 32

Baruth, Leroy, 64
Bates, Marilyn, 98-99
Bateson, Gregory, 62, 97, 114
Beauty as part of education, 46-49
Becker, Ernest, 18
Beethoven, Ludwig van, 89
Behavior
  alienation, 64
  distress, 93
  handling severe behavior problems, 104
  hyperactivity, 109
  negative and positive, 66
  perfectionism, 76, 77
Bell, Terrell H., 31
Berry, Thomas, 58, 59, 62
Berry, Wendell, 18, 42
Best-run companies, lessons from, 139-142, 144-145
Bhopal, 62, 177
Bible, 50
Birth control, 38
Briggs, Katheryn, 95
Bronfenbrenner, Urie, 76
Buchwald, Art, 76
Budget problems, 34, 41
Buhler, Ernst, 121-122
Building and buildings, 150-153
Burns, James MacGregor, 139, 142

Caesar, 130

Carlyle, Thomas, 25
Casals, Pablo, 47, 73
Celebration, 85–87, 103, 154, 159–160
Chernobyl, 62, 177
Chopra, Raj K., 143–146, 169
Cicero, 130
Colleges and universities, 113, 173
  admission of illiterate students by, 37
  Stanford University, 159
  Xavier University, 179
Collins, Marva, 143, 144
Compassion as practicum for justice, 118–121
Conformity, orderliness, and predictability, 27–31
Consumerism, rise of, 16–19
Cooking, 162
Copernicus, 112
Council Bluffs, Iowa school system, 143–144, 169
Creative learning environments, developing, 99–103
Creativity, attitude of, 83–85
Credentialing, 169–173
Culture, 2–3, 9
  and dualism, 5–6, 36, 49
  exposure in high school, 61, 62
  foreign languages, 103
  Gene Marine on, 47
  legacy of cultural pathology, 5–19
  leisure as basis of, 49
  Thomas Carlyle on, 25
  See also Art; Music
Curriculum, 68–69, 156
  revolutionizing, 111–138
  running building as part of curriculum, 152

Dante, 48
Darwin, Charles, 112
Day care and parenting centers, 120
de Chardin, Teilhard, 114
Definitions
  admiration, 72
  allurement, 51
  art, 12
  celebration, 85
  cum patior, 118
  differently-abled, 106–107
  educare, 21, 138
  expectations, 39
  government, 111
  leisure, 49
  nurturance, 63
  peer facilitator, 71
  play, 80
  power, 30
  renewal, 54–55
  responsibility, 56
  reverence, 53
  transformational leaders, 142
  wonder, 78–79
Descartes, René, 6–7
Dialogue, 24, 27
  peers, dialogue between, 88
  sex education, dialogue in, 38
Differently-abled students, 103–109
Dinkmeyer, Don, 67, 70, 91, 106, 107, 109
Drama, 120, 130
Dreikurs, Rudolf, 74, 75, 96
Driving
  drunk driving, 88
  educational class in, 89–90
  speeding, 91
Drug and alcohol abuse, 38, 60, 88
  television portrayal of, 125
Dualism, 11, 80, 97
  and culture, 5–6, 36, 49
  disease of, 5–12
  education, dualistic perception of, 114

INDEX

European dualisms, 7
  ingrained effect, 14, 15

Earth, stewardship for, 111–121, 128
Eckhart, Meister, 47, 179–180
Eckstein, Daniel, 64
Edison, Thomas E., 124
Effective Schools and Classrooms, 137
Einstein, Albert, 11, 56, 108
Ellington, Duke, 89
Encounter with the Self, 87
Encouragement, 74–78
Erney, Tom, 71

Faneuil Hall, Boston, 163
Ferguson, Marilyn, 113, 114, 139
"Five New Basics," 43
Food programs, 34
Fortune Five Hundred, 75–76
Fox, Matthew, 18, 19, 53, 56, 59, 80, 85, 118–119
Freire, Paulo, 22, 24, 27, 98, 139
Freud, Sigmund, 8

Galileo, 11, 21, 112
Glenn, Stephen, 87, 88
Global and community resources, utilizing, 178–180
Goethe, Johann Wolfgang von, 71, 129
Grades and tests, 39–40, 44
  implementing change in, 158–161
  pressures, 76, 99–100
  underachievers, 108
Gregorc, Anthony F., 96
Gregory, Dick, 49
Gymnastics, 132

Hamachek, Donald E., 74–75, 87

Handicapped students. *See* Differently-abled students
Handwork, 131–132
Handyperson programs, 120
Hayden, Tom, 145
Healing and wholeness, 21–44
High schools
  average achievement of students, 37
  exposure to different cultures in, 61, 62
  leadership roles, 119
Hippocrates, 96
Holocaust, 106
Holt, John, 10, 15, 27, 46, 81, 93, 134, 136, 170, 172
Home Educators Newsletter, 135
Homework, 39
Horney, Karen, 18
Housing rehabilitation, 119
How Children Learn, 15
Howe, Elias, 11
Human family, 116
Human interactions, 117
Hurd, Paul, 37

Illich, Ivan, 80, 127, 161–162
Industrial Revolution, 2, 44
Industry, education as, 12–16
International Year of the Child, 87
IQ scores, 108

Jantsch, Erich, 10, 12, 115
Jung, Karl, 95

Kalellis, Peter M., 90
Keen, Sam, 65, 78, 79, 84
Keeshan, Robert J., 66, 76
Kennedy, President John F., 113
Kiersey, David, 98–99
Kindergarten, 84, 100
Kirschenbaum, Howard, 158, 160

Language of form, 122-123
Languages
    classical languages, study of, 131
    foreign languages, understanding, 103
Lao-tse, 140
Leadership, transforming, 139-147, 149, 160-161
Leisure, 34, 49-51
Liedloff, Jean, 68, 74, 93
"Love and the Cabbie," 76

McKay, Gary, 67, 70, 91, 107, 109
McLuhan, Marshal, 177
Making a Bad Situation Good, 145
Management of educational system, 161-167
Marine, Gene, 47
Maslow, Abraham, 7, 13-14
Mathematics, 130
May, Rollo, 46, 83
Mead, Margaret, 113
Megatrends, 141
Merton, Thomas, 117
Middle ages, 128
Minority youth, 36, 44
Motivation, 43-44, 158
Moustakas, Clark, 92
Mozart, Wolfgang A., 11, 48
Muller, Robert, 53, 111-113, 115, 121, 179
Music
    Beethoven versus Ellington, 89
    community choruses, 120
    Mozart, 11, 48
    musical instruments, 118
    opera, 135
    study by secondary school students, 131
    time for teaching, 123
Myers, Isabel, 95

Myrick, Robert D., 71

Naisbitt, John, 141
Napier, Rodney W., 158, 160
Nation at Risk Report, 31-44
National Commission on Excellence in Education, 33-44 *passim*
National Institute of Education, 138
Neill, A. S., 82, 92, 124
Networking for cooperation, 117-180
New paradigm for learning, 149-176
New York Times, 133
Newton, Isaac, 112
Nixon, President Richard M., 180
Nuclear Regulatory Commission, 18, 42

Odyssey, The, 130-131
Otis, James, 163
Ovid, 130

Parents, 23, 38, 120, 140-141
Pascal, Blaise, 124
Pearce, Joseph Chilton, 178
Pecaut, Linnus, 108
Peers
    dialogue between, 88
    learning from, 40
    peer facilitators, 71
    Positive Educational Experiences in Relationships, 71, 165
    peer-match teachers, 127
Penick, John E., 157
Pepsi generation, 18
"Peter Principle," 161
Peters, Thomas J., 140, 141
Photography, 118
Physics, 131
Pieper, Joseph, 49-51

INDEX

Pilon, Grace, 100, 102, 178
Planned Parenthood, 38
Plato, 49, 130–131
Play, attitude of, 80–83
Poll of school superintendents, 1
Postman, Neil, 25, 84, 136
Private and parochial schools, 42, 162
Progressive Education, 72
Property taxes, 167–169
Psychology
    Alfred Adler's school of, 76
    change in psychology course, 159
    educational system, psychological foundation for, 63
    "function" or "psychological" types, 95
    Workshop Way, utilizing, 178–179
Public confidence in schools, 1
Puritan ethic, 40, 80
Pythagoras, 123

Querido, René M., 96, 122–125

Renaissance, 31
Renoir, Pierre Auguste, 48
Responsibility, 56–62
Reuther, Rosemary, 27
Reverence, renewal, and responsibility, 52–62
Richards, Mary Caroline, 57, 81, 114, 117–118
Rigden, John, 10–12
Riley, Sue Spayth, 82, 89, 94
Rogers, Carl, 22, 70

Salisbury, Harrison and Hiram, 133–134, 136–137
SAT scores, 84
School board, role of, 164–167
Science, 128, 157

"Search for Excellence in Science Education, 157
Senior citizens, health care for, 119
Sexuality, 38, 68
Simon, Sidney B., 98, 158, 160, 171
Soviet Union, 113
Spolin, Viola, 89–90
Sputnik, 34, 37, 113
Standing By Words, 42
Starhawk (author), 17, 30, 50
Steiner, Rudolf, 65, 114–115, 122, 126, 128, 129, 130, 178
Stepford Wives, The, 28–29
Stevens, John O., 24
Stevenson, Robert Louis, 11
Suicide, 88
Swimme, Brian, 52, 58, 80, 112
Systematic Training for Effective Parenting, 120

Teachers
    advising new teachers, 70–71
    co-teachers and shared learning, 153–156, 164, 171–172
    credentialing, 169–173
    educator in-service and staff development, 173–176
    influence of, 30
    peer-match teachers, 127
    recruiting, 1
    salaries, 42
    strikes, 41
    student teachers, 170, 171
Television
    bad effects of, 81
    children's TV shows, 125
    commercials, 18, 81
    evangelists, 49–50
    students' attitude toward, 28
Temperaments, honoring, 95–99

Ten key areas, implementing change in, 150–176
Terkel, Studs, 160
Tests. *See* Grades and tests
Textbooks, 157–158
Thomas, Lewis, 17
Thoreau, Henry David, 140
Three Mile Island, 177
Time, dimension of, 116
To a Dancing God, 65
Toffler, Alvin, 177
Tolstoy, Lev Nikolaevich, 48
Touch, 67–69
Trust, 69–72
Turner, Frederick, 6, 57

Universities. *See* Colleges and Universities
"Universities of the streets," 120, 162

Vandalism, 153, 167
Virgil, 130
Wad-Ja-Get?, 158, 159

Waldorf system of education, 65, 114, 128, 160, 178
Wallace, Mike, 143
Walton, Francis X., 108
Ward, Helen B., 96
Waterman, Robert H., Jr., 140, 141
Weingartner, Charles, 25, 84, 136
Western civilization, 2–3
Westside Preparatory Academy, 143
White, Naomi, 72
Whitehead, Alfred North, 28
Wonder, attitude of, 78–80
Working, 160
Workshop Way, 100–102, 178–179
World Health Organization, 87

Yager, Robert E., 157
Young children and adolescents, 121–132

Zimbardo, Philip, 159